C000177381

YACHTING
MONTHLY

A cruising anthology

A collection of true sailing stories of the sea

With an introduction
by *Maurice Griffiths*

First published in 1991 by
YACHTING MONTHLY
IPC Magazines Ltd, King's Reach Tower,
Stamford Street, London SE1 9LS

© IPC Magazines Ltd, 1991

Book editor Paul Gelder
Production editor Peter Nielsen
Book design Simon Firullo
Cover design and line drawings by Trevor Ridley
Charts drawn by Tony Garrett

Price £7.50

ISBN 1-85277-071-6

Typeset by Ebony, Heathlands Ind Est, Heathlands Road,
Liskeard, Cornwall PL14 4DH

Printed and bound by Clifford Frost Ltd, Lyon Road,
Windsor Avenue, Wimbledon, SW 19 2SE

Contents

Introduction

by *Maurice Griffiths*

For over sixty years, since 1926 when a change of policy was introduced under a new editor, Yachting Monthly has been essentially a cruising magazine; indeed, it has long been affectionately known as the 'Yachtsman's Bible'.

This anthology of cruising incidents can be said to represent some of the best of YM yarns. The yachts concerned are almost without exception up-to-date cruising boats, and their crews mainly amateur sailing men and women.

To show how the scene has changed, Ronnie Andrews gives us an insight into the ways of cruising fifty or more years ago. Then the heavily built wooden yachts, with their deep hulls, gaff rig and heavy gear, their harsh sheets and halyards, with no winches to ease the hands, and the owner's constant concern for his cotton sails and their liability to mildew and rot, were all an inseparable part of yachting.

They could be in many ways great and happy sailing days, but unblinkered old hands will also recall the leaks in an old hull fighting bad weather, and the ever present smell of damp in the

Introduction

mahogany panelled saloon and its settees, caused by poor ventilation and persistent drips through decks and hatches. The cabin sole awash and the labour at the deck pump on a hard beat to windward was an all too frequent adjunct to cruising in those 'good old days'.

Despite such troubles with many of old-time cutters and yawls, their Corinthian owners, as they were then known, made some impressive cruises, as Ronnie Andrews records. But a cruise to the Baltic and back, round Ireland, to the Mediterranean or the Azores was hailed as outstanding and somewhat risky, and usually appeared as a log-yarn in *Yachting Monthly*.

The growth of long distance voyages has become so widespread in the past few decades that crossing the Atlantic and cruising to the Pacific islands is hardly worth a Press mention. Even accounts of circumnavigations go unrecorded these days, and it has become more fashionable to say how *many* times you and your little ship have girdled the earth!

This revolution in world sailing, practised by all the yachting nations of the earth, has largely been possible through the development of mass-produced GRP hulls, from the late 1950s onwards. Thousands of owners would never otherwise have been tempted to become yachtsmen and bring with them an enormous fillip to the yachting business and all its allied trades.

It was to meet this demand for safe, short-handed sailing with labour-saving devices that inventive brains introduced the vane self-steering gear. This alone made ocean voyages possible for the limited crew or singlehander. Lightweight hulls brought in lightweight spars and gear, while the labour of old fashioned points reefing has been eliminated by slab reefing - or even in-mast or boom furling - and roller reefing headsails. Electric bilge pumps, desalinisation plants for producing fresh water from the sea, solar panels to ginger up the batteries for the ship's electronics, radar, telecommunication to other ships or shore, and the marvel of Satnav navigation are all available to the yachtsman, alone or with family or friends, making blue water voyages.

For the unimaginative, given all these electronic devices, it must appear child's play for anyone to sail his yacht across the oceans or even around the world. But every now and then there comes the story of how the elements have brought their infinite might to bear and some little ship and her crew have suffered a real fight for life; and sometimes there is disaster and another yacht is lost at sea.

As an illustration of this, Kathy Webb has written here a dramatic account of the experiences she, her husband and daughter encountered in their 45ft steel cutter when, through a bureaucratic port order, they were forced to tackle the Le Maire Strait, between Tierra del Fuego and Staten Island, during the month of August. Their ordeal highlights the dangers to be faced by ships large or small in these waters in winter time.

In the frozen waters of northern latitudes Mark O'Connell, alone in his 31ft steel ketch *Piper*, relates the chilling story of being beset in pack ice on the east coast of Greenland. Only the strength of his steel hull enabled his ship to withstand the pressure and battering she received and allowed him to work free and escape.

The northern seas and their ice-bound waters seem to hold a fascination for many cruising people, for we also have Margaret Pickering's account of her cruise with her husband in their 32ft sloop to explore the remote, fog-enveloped and ice-strewn waters of Glacier Bay, Alaska. Yachts, those mostly Canadian, were not often seen in the Bay and the settlements, few and far between, helped to create a sense of remoteness of the Far North.

In warmer waters, Jack Gush and his companions have an unusual experience as castaways while delivering a 35ft sloop from Portugal to Fort Lauderdale, Florida. After an easy run across the Atlantic before a stiff Trade wind their yacht runs on to a reef on a dark night near the Bahamas. Her GRP hull is wrecked and by daylight the crew find they are on a deserted island. Their handling of this situation and how they eventually make their escape is a practical guide to others in similar straits.

Still in deep waters, the ever present danger of a member of a yacht's company going overboard is illustrated in two of these stories. Frank Mulville, who has put many leagues of salt water astern of him in Atlantic crossings, vividly describes such an experience while running in mid-Atlantic. Alan Bond describes his dilemma with his sloop *Solveig*, caught by a deepwater fishing line

Introduction

which snagged his rudder while running before a fresh wind off the coast of New South Wales.

Whilst the lure of the islands in the South Pacific, with their blue lagoons and palm-fringed beaches, is ever present to the carefree sailor, Webb Chiles offers some interesting warnings of the effect the thousands of annual visiting yachts and their crews have had on the bureaucrats in French Polynesia. In *Passing through paradise* he describes the many restrictions that the authorities have imposed on yachts, and why it is wise for the intending yachtsman to plan his voyage according to local restrictions, the period of the hurricane season and, quite importantly, the inevitable cost of it all.

Happy cruising, skipper!

Saved by dolphins

by *Tricia Peak*

The company of dolphins, especially during a lonely night watch on board a sailing boat, is very welcome. The first intimation of their presence is usually the snorting breaths they take and the splash as they fall back into the water. If you're lucky, you may hear the high whistling noise they make and be treated to a breath-taking submarine display of phosphorescent movement, like underwater fireworks, as they leave glowing trails in their wakes.

Wayne was on the ninth day of this, his first ever sea voyage on a sailing yacht, when his ears picked out the distinctive snorting sound of these friendly creatures in the water alongside *Aeolus*. He woke from his half-doze. His watch finished in 25 minutes and he stood up, shook himself, and checked the compass bearing. All was well. The sails were drawing well and *Aeolus* seemed to be roaring along.

He stepped out on to the side deck for a better view of the aquatic acrobats. Three large, glowing shapes burst out from under the boat, very close. This would certainly be something to tell his landlubber cronies back home. Indeed, this was the sixth time he had seen dolphins this trip.

'Must be almost there,' he thought happily and sleepily. 'Wonder if there's anything to be seen ahead yet?' He peered into the darkness. What he saw sent the adrenalin surging through him. Surely it couldn't be ... but surely it was... Right ahead, there was a blacker line between the dark sky and the dark water. It could only be land. It was maybe 200 metres away. *Aeolus* was heading straight towards it.

Wayne was gripped by panic, but had the presence of mind to shout: 'Hey, can you come up here? There's land just ahead! Hey! John! Trish!'

Four scantily clad figures tumbled up the companionway into the soft tropical night of 14 degrees north.

'I was watching the dolphins, then I saw it!' Wayne was gabbling. 'There's land just there!' He gripped the wheel tightly and grimly, unable to turn it, or make any other move, as if freezing the present moment could avert the impending tragedy.

I jumped out of the cockpit to see clearly beyond the doghouse and cockpit awning. Oh my God! He wasn't wrong! The black line seemed to be no more than 100 metres away. It was hard to estimate, but it was horrifyingly close, and *Aeolus* was flying along, straight towards it.

Moreover, these shores were no sand-banks, such as the ones in the Gambia River, where we'd recently gone aground so harmlessly, Here was hard, unforgiving rock. Even the 6mm steel hull of *Aeolus* would not appreciate such an encounter.

*   *   *

We were on our way from Banjul, in Gambia, on the West Coast of Africa, to Porto da Praia on Sao Tiago, one of the most southeasterly of the Cape Verde Islands. The overall distance from Banjul to Praia is barely 400 miles, but we had already taken eight and a half days. This was due to weed growth below the water-line, after four months of the rich, unpolluted water of a wet season in the River Gambia, plus light or non-existent winds and an adverse south-setting current, against which we were constantly fighting in our effort to keep a north-west heading.

As our teenage children – our usual competent crew – were

spending a term back in Britain being educated, we decided to take on crew. This was to be our first serious encounter with the problems inherent in taking on inexperienced crew members since we started cruising two and a half years ago. Temporary crew members we've sailed with on other legs of our journey have always had previous experience. But the Gambia is not a major staging post for cruising boats, and it's not easy to find crew. When we met three easy-going, pleasant and fit-looking young Antipodeans, Andy, Rod and Wayne, who were keen to come with us, we decided that enthusiasm countered lack of experience.

We are renowned among our friends for our *Aeolus* Endurance Holidays. Any of them who read this will know what I mean: unexpected storms, 'losing' children ashore, groundings, engine failure, among other things, have enlivened our shared trips. Of course, such mini disasters are the bread and butter of sailing and cruising. It is probably this very factor of risk, excitement and unpredictability which keeps us all at it, despite the many and masochistic discomforts. Certainly, most landlubbers, those who aren't hooked on the sport, are convinced we're all quite mad.

But this particular voyage had, so far, been very tame. The odd dolphin or pilot whale, a bit of international cuisine, the completion of a few thick novels. The boys darkened their suntans on the foredeck. I skulked in the shade and pondered life after 40. John caught a dorado, a bonito and some squid. Night watches, of two hours each, had passed peacefully, with the company of a Walkman, or books read by the light of a very dim night light, while *Aeolus* steered herself.

We have Aries wind-vane steering, but only need to use it for downwind sailing. We also have an Autohelm 6000, which uses a lot of power, so we only use it when we are motoring.

The days – and the miles – slipped past. By this ninth day the wind had freshened. We bashed into the seas. No seasickness, thank goodness. But there were a couple of headaches: both John and I had one. It happened to be Rod's birthday. It was also Guy Fawkes Day, 5 November. By 1700 hours John's headache had turned into a migraine, to which he is prone, and he was vomiting. The rest of us sat down to a birthday cake I had concocted

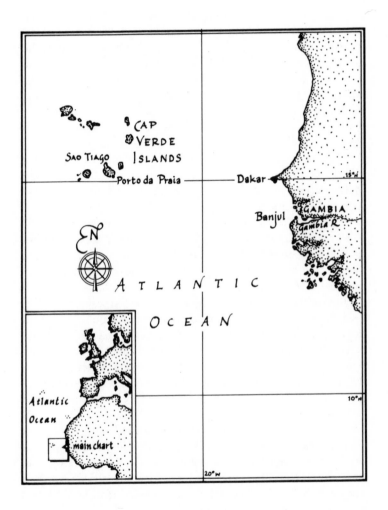

and some Sangria I dug out of a locker. Wayne cooked a very tasty omelette and we pressure-cooked some potatoes. No fireworks, I'm afraid.

A satnav fix put us 30 miles due east of Sao Tiago and south east of the island of Maio. Much excitement. Almost there! We started watching out for land, but it was slightly hazy, and by the time it grew dark at about 1930, we had seen nothing. Maio should have been about 15 miles off our starboard beam. One could only assume that the chart was accurate. We did wonder slightly, upon reading a note higher up the same chart: 'According to later determinations by the Portuguese Government, Boa Vista lies about one and three-quarter miles further eastwards.'

The satnav now decided that all the available satellites were too low in the sky and refused to give us another fix for the rest of the evening. Or perhaps our power supply was too low. These wonderful electronic aids do have their limitations.

I did a DR, based on our speed up to now. An average of 2½ to 3 knots. That gave us an ETA of 0300 hours. I hunted out our up-to-date book of lights and a chart of harbour plans for the Cape Verdes. We have radar and an RDF. There shouldn't be any problem...

But we had just spent four months in West Africa and the only light we had seen working on that coast was the one at Cap Vert, near Dakar, though many lights are actually marked on older charts. According to hearsay, the lights on the buoys and elsewhere get stolen and the authorities either don't bother to replace them or can't afford to. Moreover, buoys and navigation marks of any sort are rare, although there is a line of six buoys marking the deep-water channel into Banjul.

Had we come straight from the Canaries and Europe, it probably wouldn't have crossed our minds that the lights marked on the charts might not exist. But in this case, the question in our minds was: were the Cape Verdes sufficiently African for their European-style navigation aids to have ceased to function? We had no way of knowing the answer.

Unknown to us, although the answer was 'yes, the lights on Sao Tiago *were* still there and functioning', we were approaching in the invisible sector between the two lights.

By 2130 hours there was still no sign of land. The brightness of the half-moon seen through a haze was confusing, making the looms of any lights difficult to see.

I decided that we should reduce sail, to slow us down. We would take in the mizzen and the jib, leaving only the cutter staysail and the reefed main. Wayne helped me to put away the mizzen sail. Then we turned our attention to the jib.

I should emphasise here that my head was throbbing and I wasn't thinking very straight. John had bought the roller reefing system second-hand and had fitted it himself. I had a continuous loop of rope for winding it out and in again. In the dark I failed to see that the other end of the sheet had caught around a cleat, with the result that the line parted at the splice.

My head was still throbbing. Wayne should be all right alone in the cockpit, I reasoned. Even an inexperienced person can spot a light, or the loom of a light. By then John or I, or perhaps both of us, would be sufficiently recovered to be of some use. The boys and I decided that we would take two and a half hour watches, to let John have a break. I went below to try to sleep off my headache for a couple of hours.

At this point I made one of those dangerous assumptions: that Wayne would call us when he saw a light. It didn't occur to me to tell him to do this. Naturally, anyone with any sense, knowing they were uninformed themselves, would fetch someone who was more expert. Wouldn't they?

The time was 2200 hours. Shortly afterwards, Wayne spotted a light. He had been filling in the log at the end of watches, but it didn't occur to him to note the sighting in the log. The loom must have been visible earlier, but confused with the moon, which was in the same part of the sky.

The light Wayne saw turned out to be an ordinary town light from Porto da Praia, which was just over the hill. At least we had arrived at the right island, that is to say, the one we had been aiming for.

Wayne didn't call us. Being a thoughtful lad, he didn't want to disturb our sleep. He would manage! As far as I know, he did not check the chart, or only insofar as to make the assumption that we were headed for the channel between Sao Tiago and Maio. How

he arrived at this conclusion is hard to tell, but, certainly, there were no visible lights straight ahead of us.

*   *   *

When Wayne shouted, we came and saw - and had a fit. 'Turn the wheel!' Disaster could only be minutes, maybe seconds away. Every instant was vital. 'Turn the wheel!' John grabbed it from the rigid figure, and spun it desperately.

Fortunately, this wasn't a lee shore. The wind was on our starboard beam. Luckily, we had furled the mizzen. With this sail up, *Aeolus* usually stubbornly refuses to either tack or gybe. Even so, *Aeolus* seemed to take an inordinate amount of time to respond. In the meantime, we were inexorably steaming towards that menacing black line... The sails were stretched drum tight, the hull slicing smoothly through the water despite our underwater garden . . .

But at last there was the telltale clatter and flapping as we went through the wind, and then the sails filled from the other side, and we were pounding out of danger.

Distances are hard to judge at night and one's eyes are playing tricks. Our radar, five minutes after disaster had been averted and we were sailing away from catastrophe, showed the land to be less than a quarter of a mile away.

So what lessons did we learn?

Friends have said, 'But if there had been just the two of you, one of you two would have had to be on watch. So why not now, as you approached land?'

Yes, of course. But we did have crew. Only a singlehander has the luxury of trusting no one but himself – and even he has to sleep sometimes.

A week later I was reading Thor Heyerdahl's *Ra Expeditions*. He talks about the unpredictable currents round the Cape Verdes. Certainly, something like this could have accounted for our sudden increase in logged speed, from the average 2½ knots we had been doing to over 4. Here I have to admit, rather shamefacedly, that yes, we did have a Pilot book of the area, but no, we didn't use it. Amongst librarians it is a given truth that any information system is only as good as its retrieval system.

The third warning lesson concerns illness on board. Illness, even something as minor as a headache, is, like seasickness and getting very cold and wet, dangerous. It can warp judgement and decrease alertness at a time when these two assets are essential. I don't like taking any sort of medicament, unless it's absolutely necessary. In this case I think it was necessary. I should have waived my 'no pills' rule and dived into the medical chest for a paracetamol.

My fourth point is that vexed one of inexperienced crew. Don't forget that we had already been at sea for eight days at this point, which means that the three young men had each done eight night-watches, including writing up the log at the end of each watch. Also, at various times, I had seen each of them taking an interest in where we were on the chart. So I assumed that their common sense in this regard was greater than it really was. Always a problem of leadership this, knowing what other people have in their heads! In addition, I suppose I hadn't taken into account the fact that only the first of these eight days had involved any sort of coastal navigation. Next time we have crew who have never sailed before, I think we will get them to plot some courses and take an active interest in the chart, right from the beginning.

A final point is about me as stand-in skipper, not a role I normally take. I personally believe that the usual crew of a boat - especially if it's a cruising boat as ours is – should have the chance to be skipper, in controlled conditions, with everyone else on hand to lend moral support. Then in an emergency, any person having to take charge is more likely to make the right decision. Confidence is a vital factor in handling a boat.

I have saved my last word for the dolphins. As they are well-known for being one of the friends of mankind, it is tempting to believe that they saw our impending danger and were attempting to warn us of it! Certainly, they succeeded. And how grateful we are for the witting or unwitting part they played in our escape.

Tricia Peak is a librarian by profession and set off three years ago to sail 'slowly' around the world with her family – husband John and two children, Matthew and Emily – in Aeolus, a 14m steel ketch built in Germany.

Rays 'n rescue

by *Maurice Griffiths*

T he little barge yacht from Leigh bustled along the Foulness shore before the freshening southwesterly wind that was already flecking the distant Swin with hurrying white horses. On a short painter she was towing her substantial 10ft dinghy with its old Watermota outboard motor still clamped to the transom.

The two young fellows aboard – John, aged 17, and his brother Wilf, two years younger – were raring to make this a great holiday on their own as their father had been unable to join them this time. And they had dutifully heeded his final words to keep the outboard's sparkplug in the cabin and in the dry.

As there was not enough water yet on this tide, even for their 2ft draught, to nip through Havengore Gut into the Roach, they decided to carry on over the Maplins, to fetch up for the night off Shore Ends under the lee of Foulness Island.

The night was dark and blustery, and when they turned out soon after daybreak the ebb was away and they would soon be on the ground. But it was comparatively quiet under the lee of the point and it might be better, they decided, to stay where they were and have a good breakfast and let the barge settle on the hard sand, instead of fighting their way into the Crouch against the strong ebb.

A heavier squall came roaring over the sedge grasses of the sea wall, bringing with it rain that began to blot out the white crests on the river hurrying away seaward. It was at this savage moment, as Wilf was lighting the primus, that the dinghy's painter parted at the stem ring, and the little boat started to be swept away before their horrified eyes.

'I'll get it,' cried John, as he cast off his clothes to underpants and vest and dived in. For a time Wilf watched his brother pulling strongly at the oars, but realized the dinghy was steadily losing ground. Without hesitation he too threw off his outer clothes, dived in and joined his skipper in the boat.

At first, with an oar each, they began to make up against the seas and the tide, then with a cry John fell back when his oar snapped in the crotch and they were too horrified to speak. But they could just see their yacht disappearing in the rain with the sparkplug keeping dry in the cabin and the useless chunk of iron clinging to the boat's transom.

And there was not another boat to be seen that day, whether yacht or smack or spritty barge; not in weather like that.

*   *   *

That wild and wet morning Bill, my trusty shipmate, and I were lying at anchor in the shelter of the Roach. In the past few days we had explored the Crouch as far as Hullbridge and toured the creeks and islands inside Foulness and Wakering, and by next day we wanted to get *Storm* back in the Blackwater. With her straight stem, transom stern and under 3½ft draught, my sturdy little bawley cutter was well suited to these creeks and swatchways of the Thames Estuary.

Dawn had come up slowly, raining hard and the sou'westerly still blowing gustily. For the Blackwater it would be a fair wind, it was true, but we debated over breakfast whether to put the little old black cutter to the test in this sort of weather.

But that August of 1924 had already been generally boisterous and with the energy of youth we decided we would not sit under the lee of the sea wall all day, but as Bill said, 'git up an' go!' The

ebb had been running for two hours already and if we delayed any more there would be little water through the Ray Sand channel. Under close-reefed main and small jib, set smack-fashion halfway along our long bowsprit, *Storm* roared down towards Shore Ends and began to feel the uneasy heave of the estuary.

'That's a boat, isn't it, on the sands there,' said Bill, pointing as he handed me the glasses. It was but a dark speck away there to starboard, sitting with her mast bolt upright against the stormy sky.

'Guess she's a little barge,' I remarked. 'Anyway, she won't come to any harm there under the lee of Foulness. They'll probably have her off on the next flood in a few feet of water.'

We waved as we slid past, but nobody answered.

A heavier squall than ever blasted the backs of our oilskins with driving rain. It blotted out the view all round, but we had already caught a glimpse of the West Buxey buoy as it lifted fitfully over the seas. With a heavy gybe we were able to straighten up for the Rays'n, our shallow channel between the Essex shore to port and the four-mile expanse of the Buxey Sands to seaward. With this strong ebb it would be a downhill run to the Batchelor Spit, the next turning point into the Blackwater.

We spotted them about half way through the Rays'n; a small boat lifting and disappearing amongst the welter of the seas and rain. 'There's somebody waving an oar!' Bill's excitement was infectious.

'Right, Bill. There's a ten fathom piece of stout warp in that locker. Make one end fast to the foot of the horse and have the other ready to cast them.'

As *Storm*, with helm down, swept round close to windward of the boat, we could see it was a sizeable yacht's dinghy, half waterlogged with two young men aboard and an outboard on the stern. But what struck us most was that the bedraggled figures appeared to be in only their underpants.

This was no time for speculation, however, for I had misjudged *Storm*'s turning circle in those seas, and had to stand away for another run in. Seeing us let draw the jib and sheer off, a heart-rending wail came from both fellows.

'We'll not desert you!' I hollered. 'Keep bailing!'

With a crashing gybe – thank heaven the old boat's gear is

strong, I thought – we came in for another approach, but to my chagrin we were again just too far off for Bill to heave his line, while the younger of the two fellows appeared to have collapsed over the midship thwart. I could see that the boat appeared to have only a foot or so of frayed painter.

'Catch our warp as we come round next time,' I yelled. 'Make it fast round your for'ard thwart.' And to Bill I added, 'Let's have a sounding, old man. We must be well over the sands, but I can't see the beacon.'

Bill was prompt with the lead, and I distinctly heard the thud as it struck the hard sand. 'Not more than four feet, skipper,' he said calmly, but he knew as well as I how close we must be to striking the ground between crests.

I *must* make it this time, I thought to myself, as we stood in once more to our casualty; and *Storm*, bless her stout little heart, obeyed and laid herself almost alongside the other. They caught our line and dutifully turned it round the forward thwart, and started to haul in.

'No!' I shouted. 'Go aft. We've got to haul you out to deeper water. Keep bailing again.'

Bill was pointing through the rain. 'Look, there's the beacon.' The tall black post, with its crossroads topmark, appeared mistily through the rain and spray to leeward. (Today, it is a steel platform erection with north cardinal cones topmark – and without the inevitable cormorant).

Soon we were back in the channel, with the two dinghies towing astern, and were now able to heave to and get the fellows alongside. The younger had to be hauled aboard, for he was blue with cold and had to be almost carried into the cabin. The dinghies were eased astern in tandem, the heavier well astern, for it still had a lot of water in it. I bore away from the Batchelor Spit, while Bill attended to our casualties below, as I could guess from the volumes of smoke blowing to leeward from the stove chimney.

In due course his cheery face came out of the cabin.

'They're tucked up in blankets and fast asleep,' he said. 'I've given them hot cocoa and hung their clothes up to dry by the fire.'

Then he regaled me with their story of how they went boating on such an unpleasant day in their underwear with an

outboard motor that wouldn't work, and how they daren't drop it overboard to lighten the dinghy because the barge yacht was their dad's pride and joy.

I couldn't help shuddering to think what would have happened if no one had come along and picked them up. The lads would have drifted on the ebb before ever increasing seas into the Wallet and towards the coast between Colne Point and Clacton. But in their exhausted condition I doubted if they could have kept afloat much longer.

With the dinghies in tow, *Storm* thrust her way up against the Blackwater ebb. The rain had ceased and a cold looking sun was glinting on the surface of the river as we entered the Quarters and picked up a mooring in Thornfleet Channel, almost opposite the Hard.

After a good hot meal, our young friends were fully recovered and anxious to get back to Burnham to find a yard to help them collect their little ship. Their exuberance was infectious, for their 'smalls' were almost scorched dry by the stove, and while we decked them out in what outer clothes had to spare and lent them enough cash for their bus and train fares, Bill and I almost fell against each other at young Wilf's appearance in Bill's ample pea jacket, trousers and old deck shoes, all several sizes too big for the lad. From their laughter, as they paddled their dinghy to the Hard with an oar and floorboard, it was clear they had suffered no harm from their experience.

We met them a few days later in the Blackwater on a breezy day, still full of high spirits, with no reefs in and bumping along with their weather chine a foot or more out of the water. They brought up near us off Osea, to return the clothes and cash they had borrowed, and described how good the longshoremen at Burnham had been in helping them fetch their barge from Foulness not in the least damaged.

'We've been in the news,' beamed John, handing us a crumpled copy of the Southend Standard. There was the heading: 'Yachtsmen's Gallant Rescue in North Sea Gale' above a story about the Rays'n incident. They were now, they said, on their way on the next ebb to explore the Orwell.

'And when we get home,' piped young Wilf, 'we're going to

try to persuade dad to sell the old barge – she's much too slow –
and buy a Leigh cockler, or a ship more like your *Storm!*'

And that was, bless my soul, some sixty-seven years ago, and
I've often wondered since if they ever got their wish, for I never
met them again.

*Maurice Griffiths celebrated his 89th birthday in 1991. From his
drawing board he has launched nearly 2,000 little ships afloat
around the world - and more than 140 designs. As the author of
books like* The Magic of the Swatchways, *he has lured generations
into creeks and silent backwaters. He was editor of* Yachting Monthly
*for 40 years and now lives with his wife, Marjorie, in West Mersea on
the Blackwater, scene of so many evocative episodes in a rich life of
sailing and writing about boats.*

Passing through paradise

by *Webb Chiles*

Jill and I were aboard *Resurgam*, our 36ft sloop, in which we had just spent a ridiculously rough night after an otherwise slow and gentle passage from Nuku Hiva. Our engine had died some months earlier in Panama, so we just sat.

From time to time cat's-paws gently touched the water and we turned *Resurgam*'s bow toward the pass through the reef, but each time, before we approached too closely, the wind disappeared and the ocean resumed her glassy face.

Once, just before the Christmas of 1974, I had almost lost another boat, one without an engine, when the wind died in Papeete pass and the current started to carry me on to the reef. I was saved then by an approaching line squall. The experience made me, if not more cautious, then at least more sceptical. I wanted wind I could believe in before we sailed through the reef, though a few weeks later we were to enter another pass with a breeze weaker than a butterfly's cough.

After four hours, we saw the water darkening out by Venus Point; then the darker patches spread and became one and moved towards us. We unfurled the jib and trimmed the main. By the time an 8 knot breeze reached *Resurgam* we were squared off for the pass and the boat speed indicator leapt from zero to 5 knots.

Papeete Pass appears deceptively narrow, although I have watched the QE2 enter. The reef comes almost vertically off the seabed. A hundred yards outside, our sounder, which starts reading at more than 700ft, showed no bottom. Then Jill called, '720.' A moment later, she said, '42,' and waves were breaking on either side of us and a few yards away a Tahitian was standing in water that barely reached his knees. Then it was '90' and we were through. Just in time, too.

We both know Tahiti. This was the fifth time I had sailed there since 1974, and Jill and I had been together there in 1985; Jill was closing the circle of her first circumnavigation at the moment we sailed through the pass. Still, I like to be certain we are both thinking ahead and anticipate as much as possible what we are both going to do. We expected wind changes near the hills behind the town. It was a week after Bastille Day and we hoped that some of the cruising boats would have moved out. We would furl the jib and then tack along the waterfront, deciding on where we could best fit in, gybe, and sail back to place our anchor, and then, depending on the wind, row our stern lines ashore.

Halfway across the harbour, several things happened. We furled the jib; the wind died; our speed dropped from 5 knots to 1½; the chimes on the green-roofed protestant church struck noon; and thirty small, gaily-painted, noisy, overpowered speedboats roared away from the quay and headed for us at speed. You either give up the sea, or you become a fatalist. There was certainly no way we could get out of their way, so we sat there nearly becalmed and hoped all the drivers were looking. Like a swarm of wasps, they approached us and, at the last moment, separated, passing on either side, before turning and roaring back to the quay to see if they could come closer the next time.

We were in the middle of a race. After lap two, a launch containing the port captain puttered out. 'You are not supposed to be here,' he said. Somehow we had already guessed that. 'Our engine is broken. We are moving as fast as we can.' The swarm approached, deafened us, and left us tossing in its wake. 'Where are you coming from?' 'Nuku Hiva,' we replied. At this he relaxed. He shepherded us to the end of the line of moored boats, where we simply dropped the main and our anchor. So much for plans; so much for carefully evaluating the possibilities and choosing our spot.

I do not like Mediterranean-style moorings, anchor down and stern lines ashore, which the officials insist you use in Papeete. But if there was no wind to set our anchor, there was also no wind to worry about pushing us ashore. Not the rest of that Saturday; nor all of Sunday. Not until Monday morning, when we were ashore handling the necessary paperwork, did any wind return, and then it was only about 20 knots from the east. We were in the bank when we noticed the palm trees swaying outside. When, officialdom placated, we returned to *Resurgam*, we found her bow had swung until she was parallel with the beach. Considering that you put your anchor down in 50ft or 60ft and the water is still 25ft deep a boat-length off the edge of the black sand, she was not in danger, and we never were certain if the Bruce had dragged, or if the sloop had simply straightened out the 150ft of anchor chain we had veered. In any event, I did something I don't like to do and rowed out our second anchor, a 35lb CQR mostly on line.

A few weeks earlier when we had sailed into Nuku Hiva, in amazement I had exclaimed, 'It is all over.' 'It' could have been my third circumnavigation, which I was completing there; but I meant cruising in the South Pacific, for where I had never before in Taiohae Bay seen more than a handful of boats, in July 1990 there were thirty. Even worse, almost all were unnecessarily anchored fore and aft, something I dislike even more than Med-style moorings. Of course, projecting such numbers to the harbours lying ahead, I knew that most would be intolerable.

Fortunately, until we reached Suva, Fiji, Nuku Hiva was the exception. Most places in French Polynesia were less crowded in 1990 than they had been in 1985. When we left Papeete in late August, 285 yachts had officially entered since the beginning of the year; a month later, we were the 187th yacht recorded at Bora-Bora. The official estimate of the number of yachts expected to enter at Tahiti for the year was only 350.

That most of the boats cruising French Polynesia in 1990 had

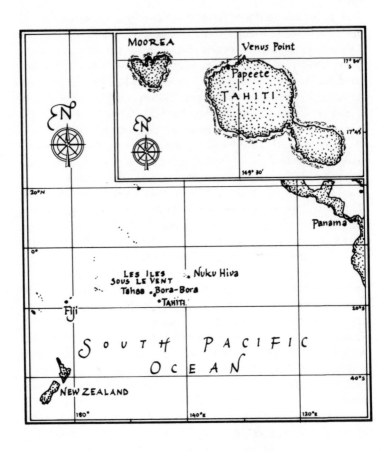

entered by August was due to a new regulation. In the gendarme's office on the Papeete waterfront, a notice in French and English stated that no visiting sailor was permitted to remain aboard his boat during the cyclone season from 1 November to 1 April, and that anyone attempting to do so would be compelled to use his bond money to fly home from Tahiti. I had heard rumours of this, and asked the gendarme who was processing our papers if it was being enforced. The reply was a firm 'Yes.'

This is unfortunate, for it means that where in the past sailors could take a year (November to November is consistent with the weather patterns) to cross from North America to New Zealand or Australia, now they would have only half that time. French Polynesia does have cyclones, several in 1983, but is not really in a high-risk area. Perhaps the regulation will be modified in practice, but any sailor would be well advised to check before starting across the Pacific during the northern winter.

Tahiti in 1990 had also become even more expensive, with several new or increased fees. The bond had been increased for Americans to 850 dollars per person, and would be proportionately higher the further from Papeete your home country is than America. The former Bank of IndoSuez has become Westpac, which charges 25 dollars per person for keeping this money without paying you any interest. Additionally, they will convert that into Polynesian francs and then convert it back when you leave, making a profit for them both times. If you do not have a visa when you arrive, one will cost 35 dollars per person in Tahiti, as will any extensions. The port entrance fee is 25 dollars, and the charge for anchoring in Papeete for a 36ft boat is three dollars per day, more than twice what it was in 1985. Add them all together and you find that it will cost a couple 200 dollars just to arrive in Papeete. And, of course, when you step ashore, the money will truly flow.

One positive change was the new EuroMarche supermarket, just south of Maeva Beach, which is the biggest between America and New Zealand. Prices are good there, by Tahitian standards, and the selection is outstanding. However, any wise sailor will still be as completely provisioned as possible when he arrives in Tahiti.

Another positive change is that in general people were friendlier in French Polynesia than they had been before. But then they should be. They are all getting rich enough.

Generally only first-timers spend much time in Papeete itself, and after a week we raised anchor and sailed over to Moorea. Unfortunately, but not unexpectedly, because new boats had come in beside us and crossed both our anchor rodes, it took a cursing hour before our anchors were free, and Jill gybed the mainsail and steered for the pass, while I struggled to clear the worst tangle of lines and chain *Resurgam*'s deck has ever known. In addition to the 150ft of chain and 200ft of line to the anchors and two 200ft stern lines, there was 200ft of new chain I had just bought to replace the old rusty and badly worn chain to our main anchor.

I had discovered the new chain at a chandlery next to the Yanmar agent, who did not have any engines in stock. The problem with the chain was that it was reasonably priced, which, in Tahiti, makes you think not that you have found a bargain, but that there must be something wrong with it. However, the Frenchman who manages the chandlery, with whom I had done business in the past, proclaimed the chain to be European manufactured, rather than Taiwanese, properly galvanised, tested etc.

Disposing of the old chain posed a problem. You don't just leave 400lbs of rust on the sidewalk for the rubbish collector, or dump it in the harbour, where some other sailor will snag it with his anchor; we dropped it in the depths on our sail over to Moorea, hopefully hitting a French submarine. The speed and force of the old chain as it roared over the roller was frightening.

Sometimes you don't realise what constant tension you live under, precisely because it is constant, until unexpectedly you relax. After complications in Nuku Hiva and Papeete, everything went just as planned as we sailed into one of our favourite anchorages in Moorea, just inside the reef on the pass into the deep cove of Opunohu, and dropped our newly chained anchor into 15ft of clear water, well away from the three other boats already there.

We spent a perfect week at Moorea, part of it storm-bound, but

Resurgam was well protected from the north-east gusts by the reef and I could swim out whenever I needed to be reassured and see the Bruce safely buried in the sand. Surprisingly, considering that we had spent most of the preceding months at sea, we hardly went ashore. It was enough to stay home together, with *Resurgam* able to swing with the wind, to snorkel over the coral formations and watch the fish, to read and listen to music. The loss of the engine would have been serious had our two solar panels not generated enough electricity to use the compact disc player for two or three hours each evening.

And, of course, we were in as beautiful an anchorage as exists anywhere. Moorea is other-worldly. The jagged, serrated ridge-line, the improbable mountain peaks, the two fjord-like bays cutting deeply into the north coast, were all made more mysterious by shifting grey clouds and tendrils of mist and rain.

After that perfect week, it took us all of one day to sail the 15 miles back to Papeete to buy some fresh provisions and check for letters. There we learned that during the storm, which was not a severe one, Papeete harbour had become a madhouse, with boats dragging into one another, taking the full force of wind on the beam. The only major damage was to a vessel which caught a line around her propeller and pulled her engine off its mounts.

We had expected to remain at Tahiti longer, but the wind had been too light to reach the anchorage around the corner from Papeete, and the Harbourmaster told us that we could not remain swinging at anchor for more than 24 hours. So we took Le Truck out to EuroMarche, bought all we could carry, and left Papeete for the Iles Sous Les Vent.

Again the wind was light, as it generally was for all of the southern winter of 1990 in the South Pacific, and we had a gentle spinnaker run overnight, finding ourselves off Huahine at dawn.

Because the only shallow anchorage is usually overcrowded, we by-passed Huahine and headed directly for Raiatea and Tahaa, 20 miles further west; but our expectation of being through one of the many passes those two islands share within their single surrounding reef by noon, vanished with the sunrise.

At noon we were not safely through a pass, but becalmed halfway between Huahine and Tahaa beneath a heavy sky. Tahaa vanished in rain and a gust of wind hit us from the west. I furled the jib and let *Resurgam* reach north, heeled far over under mainsail. We did not want to go north, but just then we also did not want to go west, where a waterspout was guarding Tahaa like a dragon.

For an hour rain fell and the wind boxed the compass. Then the rain stopped, the sky partially cleared, Tahaa reappeared four miles to the west, and the wind disappeared. We furled the jib as the sloop rolled around helplessly. Water fell on us from the slatting mainsail. Being becalmed outside passes was becoming unpleasantly familiar.

The sun and *Resurgam* oozed west. At 1700, with an hour of light left, we still had a mile to go and were making only 2 knots with the wind on the port quarter. Our boat speed was really too low to attempt the pass, but we were not yet at the point of no return and it might be as dangerous to be becalmed while trying to remain outside the reef for the night, as to chance heading in.

That pass is narrow, but clearly defined by palm trees on *motus*, or islets, on either side. A low swell was breaking lazily on the reef. Two sailing boats inside the lagoon were scurrying to reach an anchorage before the swiftly approaching darkness. They were under power. The lagoon was glassy, but then so was the sea. *Resurgam* continued to glide onward, her slight boat speed equalling the wind so that we felt as though we were becalmed. It was difficult to decide whether to commit ourselves to the attempt, or turn and try to find searoom. Our lives were not at risk, but our home and everything we own in the world was. 'You have done more dangerous things in sailboats,' I reminded myself. But then I added, '. . . not lately . . . still, you are supposed to be a sailor; this is one of the arts around which you have forged your identity.' I peered over the side. A few bubbles bobbing slowly astern proved that we were moving. Or, at least, that the water was. I lined up one of the palm trees on the nearer *motu* with a rock on Tahaa. The bearing changed. We were moving forward. I pushed the tiller away from me and then back. The bow slowly responded. 'There's risk either way,' I said to Jill. 'It depends on the wind and how much current we find in the pass.'

'Your decision,' she said.

I headed in. The current caught us near a black pole, marking the edge of the coral on the south side of the pass. For long moments we hung suspended in time and motion. Only musical ripples of the current against *Resurgam*'s burgundy hull. Polynesians in an outboard-driven launch were fishing. They waved cheerfully. Jill waved back politely.

Equilibrium was broken by the wind swinging directly to our stern, reducing its apparent force. *Resurgam* began to drift backwards. We were too close to the reef to turn to port. I told Jill to gybe the main, which was quicker than pulling the jib across. Wing and wing, the sloop slowed her sternway, held motionless again, and then eased ahead. We both held our breath.

In three or four agonising boat-lengths, the worst of the current was behind us. In the shadow of Tahaa, we sailed on to the ledge behind the northern *motu* and dropped our anchor.

'This calls for a bottle of wine,' Jill said.

'Why else do you think I came in?' I replied.

We sat in the cockpit, watching the island disappear and the stars appear in the deepening darkness. Before we finished our first glasses of wine, a strong wind came up and blew for three days.

Webb Chiles is a well known author who has been sailing for 25 years. His previous boats include Chidiock Tichborne, a Drascombe Lugger, in which he made some notable and audacious singlehanded voyages, and an Ericson 37, Egregious. Resurgam, which he sails with his wife, Jill, is a Sparkman and Stephens She 36.

Bluewater castaways

by *Jack Gush*

It was a restless sort of night. For some reason, which I could not define, I had a strong premonition that all was not well. Twice during Lella's watch from 0400 to 0600 I got up, went to the cockpit and asked her if she was steering the courses Tom had given her.

Tom, our skipper, claimed to be familiar with the area and had laid off a series of courses to take us from Ambergris Cay in the outer Bahamas, round the southern limit of the vast Caicos Bank and then north-west to Acklins Island, a passage of 200 miles.

We were delivering *Arcularius V*, a 35 ft sloop, from Vilamoura in Portugal to Fort Lauderdale, and were now nearing the end of what had been a harmonious and successful voyage.

The three of us were following our customary night watch routine, two on and four off. Normally, I had only to put my head to the pillow to fall into a deep and dreamless sleep. But that night sleep would not come.

Towards the early hours I must have dozed off. It seemed to me that I had hardly slept at all when there was a tremendous crash and a jolt from underneath that shook the yacht from truck to keelson. Then, to my relief, she seemed to sail on, but only to strike again and yet again.

As I struggled up, I could hear Lella calling for Tom from the cockpit and by the time I came into the saloon from the forward cabin his bulky figure was ahead of me, mounting the companionway steps. By this time the yacht had come to rest on her beam ends. As I climbed into the cockpit, I could hear the roar of the breaking seas. Lella had been thrown about but was not injured. The next wave sent spray all over us and the yacht lifted and then pounded, but she had stopped driving across the reef, or whatever we had hit.

The time was 0520; the moon had gone down and the night was pitch black. Tom discovered that on our lee side, where the stanchions were half awash, we were in 2ft of water. Breaking seas hit hard on the weather side of the yacht and broke over us into the cockpit. We were soon drenched, but at least the water was warm.

We were not sure what we had hit or where we were, and it was too dark to see anything. So we went below to await daylight and assess our situation. The yacht still lifted and pounded in an alarming manner, but more than half an hour was to pass before we heard the ominous cracking and splitting of the glass fibre hull. Water then started to trickle in and was soon slopping round our feet.

In the meantime we drank some rum and sent out a Mayday on the VHF, though we knew we were in a sparsely populated area and were certain our call would go unanswered.

As I perched as best I could on the upper side of the saloon in dripping oilskins, sipping the rum, I was overcome by a feeling of deep disappointment. What had been a happy voyage had ended in a shambles. Cushions, clothes, bedding and books had tumbled onto the lee side, and already Tom's bunk and much of his gear was half under water. Lella was up forward, attempting to pack our clothes into a large red canvas bag.

At the first glimpse of light, Tom and I were in the cockpit straining our eyes shorewards. Gradually we could make out the land, low-lying and sandy, about 300 yards away. We decided it must be one of the Inaguas, either Great or Little Inagua, two islands that form part of the outer Bahama group. We were on a reef on which the seas were breaking heavily. The Trade Wind was blowing steadily at 20 knots. The reef was insufficient to give much of a lee and the sea inside it was choppy.

Tom climbed gingerly over the lee rail and stood up to his thighs in the water. He decided, unwisely I thought, to try to wade ashore and make a reconnaissance. I insisted on putting a line round his waist and paying out as he went. This was just as well, for after a few yards he disappeared with the waves over his head. A raised hand appeared, which I took to be the signal to haul him back to the comparative safety of the yacht.

In all her years of sailing Lella has never learnt to swim, so it was decided that Tom should now row her ashore to terra firma in our inflatable. We could see that there was a long, sandy beach running off to the south, backed by low scrub and stunted palm trees. Before Tom left, we inflated our six-man liferaft and attached it to a stanchion that was not quite under water.

While Tom had gone, I began to gather up the gear and provisions we would need as castaways, and load them into the liferaft. At the angle at which the yacht lay, buffeted by the seas, moving about was something of an acrobatic feat and progress was slow and wet. I was concerned only with our immediate future. I collected tins of food, two 25-litre jerry cans of fresh water, a sail to serve as a tent, an awning as a groundsheet, a small camping stove, spare gas containers, plenty of lines, a ball of twine and an axe. I did not forget the tin opener, the cutlery, a sharp knife, matches, mugs, loo paper, soap, the binoculars, a torch, a few tools and some fishing gear. But I discovered later that I left behind my wallet, containing money and credit cards, though more than once my hand must have been within inches of it.

Tom returned after a hard row against wind and sea. I could see he was tired. We loaded the bag Lella had thoughtfully packed into the liferaft. The interior of the yacht was now chaotic. The water was over the batteries, which were giving off acrid fumes. We sloshed about and gathered up our documents: the ship's papers, insurance policy and our passports.

We attached the laden liferaft to the inflatable with a short line.

The inflatable was full of water from the spray that came right over the yacht, but we climbed in and while Tom rowed I bailed with a saucepan. Downwind it was relatively easy going.

On the beach we took stock of our situation. It was now daylight and we found we were on the east side of Great Inagua. The island's northern extremity, a low sandy headland, was only a few hundred yards away. The green scrub and the sprinkling of stunted palms covered the island as far as the eye could see. Just north of us, the beach ran into rocks that continued as far as the headland. The reef ran roughly north-south, parallel to the beach, about 300 yards offshore. Inside the reef were a number of nasty-looking coral heads, which became more prominent at Low Water.

We were clearly miles from anywhere, in a lonely sea-area, and it might be days before we were rescued. We began to carry the gear from the liferaft up to the scrub and organise a camp. The beach was littered with exactly the kind of bamboo poles that were needed to make the framework of a tent. The ball of twine came in handy for the lashings and the lines became guys for the tent poles.

Finally, we pulled the liferaft up to higher ground, from where we hoped its orange canopy might be spotted by a passing vessel. In it we left our scant emergency gear: a few flares, a torch and two small cans of water. The bushes round the tent soon became decorated with our wet, bedraggled clothing.

At about noon we crowded into the tent to get out of the heat. I made a salad with a few bits and pieces, but none of it was eaten. We each had a drink of water and began to discuss our situation.

The island of Great Inagua is pear-shaped and is about 65 miles long. There is one settlement, Matthew Town, at its south-ern end, near extensive saltings. We were at the northern end, the tip of the pear. The rest of the island is uninhabited.

None of us was enthusiastic about a 60-mile walk through the prickly scrub, carrying a load of provisions. The alternatives were to try to get to Matthew Town in the inflatable, or stay where we were in the camp. I seemed to remember reading somewhere that as a general rule castaways are better off to remain encamped in one place and try to attract attention.

In the afternoon, Tom rowed out to the yacht, still on the reef, to get our charts to help make a better assessment of our position. Lella and I set off with binoculars to reconnoitre our immediate surroundings and walked up to the sandy headland. We could see where the reef petered out at the point. Had our course been 50 yards to the east, we would have cleared both reef and headland and sailed between the two Inaguas. We could see Little Inagua about five miles away, also uninhabited. A current in the night setting strongly to the south-west had put us several miles off course.

We sat down and minutely scanned the interior through the binoculars for any sign of human activity, however small. About two miles away rotting trees protruded at crazy angles from a big lake or swamp, which we judged to be salt water, or at least brackish. As we walked slowly back to the camp we came across some dung, dried out but not that old. But what sort of animal? We have never before studied dung with such keen interest.

Our first night in the camp was a misery. Tom, perhaps out of respect for our privacy, chose not to sleep in the tent, but under the bushes. Lella and I lay down in our oil-skins with our other clothes as a makeshift pillow. We had thought that because the ground was sandy it would be soft, or at least yielding, but we soon found it as hard as concrete. The wind got up and swung to the north-east, so that the tent became a wind tunnel and the sail flapped noisily. The palm fronds rustled, and more than once I thought of the dung and the wild animals that must be somewhere about.

Two or three times in the night I got up and went down to the beach. I peered seawards, but there were no lights, only darkness and wind.

At dawn I found Tom standing above the beach, gazing out to sea. He had not slept either. The yacht now lay over, her mast in the water. The previous afternoon, Tom had found the cabin flooded and had been unable to rescue our charts. It looked as if we would not get much more out of her, though things that floated might get washed ashore. The tide was out and the beach was devoid of footprints. A flock of sandpipers, unafraid of humans, tripped unconcernedly across the sand, only feet away from us.

Bluewater castaways

We made coffee on the tiny stove and then moved the tent. This time we were more thorough. We chose a sheltered hollow, uprooted all the bushes and stacked them as a windbreaker and wild animal fence. We gathered palm fronds and made a mattress of them, several inches thick. We collected driftwood and made a galley protected from the wind, and with shade for our tins of food.

We calculated we had food for at least 20 days, plus 40 litres of water, which we intended to ration with great care. Though there were probably animals about, we could not count on finding fresh water.

In the afternoon I donned mask and flippers, hoping there were no sharks about. I swam lazily among the coral heads, some with rusty antlers; there were mounds of mustard-coloured brain coral three feet high; waving fans, long-spined urchins and dead men's fingers – all in a confusion of colour. And there were fish everywhere. We were not likely to die of starvation, I thought, as I swam among them. I had no gun and began to ponder the question of catching them. We had a few hooks and we had our dinghy, or perhaps I could fashion a spear.

That evening we cooked ourselves a decent meal: a tin of stew and a tin of sweetcorn. Except for our torches, which we were anxious to conserve, we had no form of lighting; so before it got dark at about 1900 the meal had to be cooked and eaten. It was not clear whether it was supper or high tea. We washed it down with sips of water.

After breakfast the next morning Tom went for a walk to explore to the south, and I set about making further improvements to the camp. Lella later went to the beach to wash the dishes in the sea. Suddenly, I heard her shouting, 'There's a ship, there's a ship!'

As I ran, it seemed an incredible stroke of good fortune that a vessel had come into these waters so soon.

But sure enough, there she was, about two miles away to the south, outside the reef, the black shape of a small ship. Lella ran to our tent and came back with a mirror. I placed her on the beach a few yards away, facing the sea, so that the ship appeared to me to sit on the top of her head. I trained the mirror until the flash fell

41

on her back and then moved it up to the top of her head, and then flashed it repeatedly up and down. After a couple of minutes I stopped and we waited, straining our eyes for any sign of response. Tom had walked along the beach in that direction. Would they see him? 'It's going further away,' Lella said, despair in her voice. I tried to line up the distant boat with some part of the reef to discern which way it was moving, but without a definite result.

I started flashing the mirror again. Watching carefully, I noticed that the ship was approaching. For the moment I said nothing to Lella; I wanted to be certain.

Then everything seemed to happen at once. We saw Tom striding back along the beach, and a small wooden boat appeared inside the reef, powered by an outboard, with two men in it, moving quickly towards us. We stared in disbelief.

Tom and the men in the boat arrived at about the same time. The two men, one inky black and the other brown, both dressed in tattered shorts, spoke Spanish; a language with which we have no difficulty.

They explained that they were from the Dominican Republic, fishing illegally in these waters. They had seen Tom on his walk and our signals, but had come to explain that they could not help us. If caught by the Bahamas police they would go to prison. The brown one stressed this by crossing his wrists, as if handcuffed.

But surely, we replied, they were not going to leave us on the beach, two men and a woman, to die of thirst.

They spoke of their poverty. They had not yet started fishing. In a few days time, with their catch, if they were lucky, they would return to Santa Domingo. They were sorry, they could not help us.

Could they take just one of us to Matthew Town, we asked.

It was a long way off, they answered. They would lose fishing time.

We replied that we would be prepared to pay their expenses.

I saw them glance towards the reef and our stricken yacht, as if to assess our financial standing. They then moved away, towards the bow of their boat, and conferred among themselves. After a few minutes they came up with their figure – five thousand US dollars.

We received this figure in stony silence. The wavelets slapped gently against our legs. I think that all of us were aware that we were about to bargain in earnest, perhaps for our lives, but we were not going to pay a ridiculous price. We put our heads together at the stern of the boat.

Our offer was for them to take Tom to within a few miles of Matthew Town at night and land him on the beach. For this we were prepared to pay 200 dollars.

They conferred among themselves for quite some time, and eventually came up with a figure of 500 dollars, a tenth of their original asking price, and as I pointed out to Tom, not a bad figure when worked out on a per person basis.

Tom went back to the camp to get ready. Lella and I stayed talking to the fishermen. We thought it wisest not to let them see our stores. I asked them about the wild animals. There were wild donkeys, they told us, hundreds of them, and they could be aggressive. We ought to watch out for them, they said. There were also wild cattle and boar.

Tom returned and we said goodbye, and they took him out, through the reef, to where their fishing boat lay rolling horribly.

Left to ourselves, Lella and I settled down to camp life. We continued to ration ourselves as regards both food and water. As I pointed out to Lella, it was not certain when, or if, Tom would return. The fishermen might not take him to Matthew Town; they might take him to Santa Domingo, in which case he would be weeks getting back to us. Or they might suspect that he had more than 500 dollars on him, which he had, cut his throat and toss him overboard.

In the days that followed there was plenty to do. Again we improved the camp and thickened up the surrounding prickly bushes, our wild donkey defence. We left the inflatable handy on the beach in case the donkeys came in force; in which case we planned to row out a short distance, on the assumption that they could not swim.

The mattress of palm fronds was now over a foot thick and was, Lella declared, as comfortable as our mattress at home. But often I could not sleep. This may have been because, without lighting, we went to bed so early. But I would lie awake, listen-

Bluewater castaways

ing to the rustling palms, and a plan began to form in my mind to get us out of our predicament if Tom failed to return.

This plan entailed cutting a path through the scrub and carrying the dinghy to the lee side, where the sea was flat calm. This would take Lella and I some time, perhaps two or three days, but we could cover the distance in stages, returning to the camp every evening. We could then sail down the lee side, anchoring or beaching the boat at night.

Our inflatable was a Tinker and could be sailed, except that its centreboard, mast, and sail, were under water in *Arcularius*. But its rudder and tiller unit had, by a stroke of luck, already been washed ashore. It would not be too difficult to make a centreboard, and, with the bamboos lying around, a mast.

Beach-combing soon became an important part of our daily routine. Early every morning and last thing before our evening meal we carefully searched the beach, and were usually rewarded for our pains. One day we found a box of a dozen eggs, which we had bought in the supermarket in San Juan, Puerto Rico, and only two were broken. Another time it was an almost full bottle of good quality Spanish olive oil, which we had transported from the Canary Islands. These were important additions to our stores.

And one evening I found one of our sails in a bag, half buried in the sand. It was *Arcularius*'s cruising chute and was of very light material, exactly what we wanted. Our escape plan in the dinghy was now beginning to materialise. I rather fancied the idea of sailing into the harbour at Matthew Town, two castaways who had struggled back to civilisation on their own initiative.

Though we did not put our plan into effect for the moment, while we waited for Tom, the idea of it buoyed our morale and we discussed it endlessly.

However, it was not to be. Three days later, early in the morning, Lella sighted a vessel. This time she walked calmly into the camp and said matter-of-factly, 'There's a white boat of some sort, lying off the headland.'

We took the binoculars and hurried along the now well-worn path. The binoculars were not necessary. A small boat had already come through the reef on the lee side of the headland, and the several people in it were now landing. Among them we could see

Tom's white-haired head.

Soon the police, armed with hefty-looking rifles, were pushing through the scrub towards us, like an assault force. Some of them were exceptionally tall and fit-looking. The local chief of police, we were to find, was among them. They were all black.

We led them to the camp where, with tongue in cheek, we said, 'Coffee, gentlemen?' To our pleasure, our invitation was readily accepted.

When the coffee was drunk, they dismantled our camp; and all our gear, now quite a considerable amount, they carried off, balanced on their heads or brawny shoulders. We did not quite realise that we were never to see most of it again.

Tom, it turned out, had not been taken to Matthew Town. The fishermen had put him ashore about 10 miles north of it, and in the night he had walked along the beach, stumbling over rocks and removing mosquitoes from his face in handfuls.

We were loaded into the small boat, which then headed towards the reef under the power of its big outboard. The breaks in the reef were, I could see, shallow and the sea was breaking heavily on them. I covered our cameras and warned Lella to hold on. We hit the gap just as a sea broke. It swept us from stem to stern and half filled the boat, to the delight of the police.

The rescue boat was called *Foxy Lady* and was a typical flybridge, sport-fishing boat, though in filthy condition. On the way to Matthew Town the skipper stopped and let her drift. With two of the police he jumped into the small boat, having first tossed in their underwater fishing gear. They zoomed off towards a dazzling beach about a mile away, and half an hour later, when they returned, in the bottom of the boat were two large lobsters and about five kilos of fish.

Once cleaned, scaled and chopped up the lot went into a blackened pot, along with tomatoes, peppers, potatoes and spices. One of the policemen, the smallest one, was cook. The result was the most delicious bouillabaisse I have ever eaten. Afterwards, sitting in the sun, watching the island slip lazily by, knowing we would soon come to Matthew Town, it was difficult to stay awake.

Bluewater castaways

*Jack Gush and his wife, Lella, now sail a 43ft steel cutter-rigged sloop,
Jackella. His first cautious sailing was some 25 years ago in the
Mediterranean. He has several ocean passages, including two
previous Atlantic crossings, to his credit. The couple sailed from
Gibraltar in 1988, via the Canaries, the Gambia, Brazil, the
Caribbean, Panama, and 'dawdled across the Pacific to arrive in the
Bay of Islands, New Zealand, in November 1990. He is retired and
adds, 'We sold up and sailed . . . with not one regret.'*

Stranger in the night

by *Bill Perkes*

A wave broke on our weather quarter in a phosphorescent glow. Then another in the same place, and another. It might be dolphins. The breaking, flashing waves were coming closer, straight for us, and appeared to be fairly regular. Too regular. It could be a whale coming to play. If it was, it was getting far too close. Whales sometimes sink yachts.

Hazel and I, in our faithful twenty-year-old sloop *Sherpa Bill*, were on our way back to Britain after a successful and enjoyable cruise which had taken us from the Isle of Wight to Madeira, the Canaries, through the Windward and Leeward Islands, north to Bermuda and on to the Azores. Nothing very exciting, in fact the normal Atlantic circuit, completed by hundreds of yachts every year.

I had promised Hazel a nice easy trip back. I had studied the North Atlantic Pilot Chart at length and was confident that we would have fair winds and a kick up the backside from the Gulf Stream.

The weather as far as Anguilla, the most northern of the

Leeward Islands, had been perfect and as per the Pilot. But then it all went horribly wrong. We should have had about three days of easterly Trade Winds from Anguilla going north, then variables up as far as Bermuda. What we got was 300 miles of calms and variables, then a northerly gale for the remaining 500 miles. Not at all pleasant. Not only that, but when we did get to Bermuda it rained very heavily and for two days there was a thick fog, a phenomenon which had not occurred for at least thirty years.

The Pilot said that from Bermuda, the winds would be favourable. No such luck. The first couple of days weren't too bad. Then we had a mini gale. Now a mini gale isn't a real gale, it's a Force 6 or 7 on the nose and very unpleasant. I don't like them (Hazel hates them).

Shortly after that, the wind went round to the north, enough to enable us to lay the course. Then it blew a real gale. A solid 40 knots for three days, with black scudding clouds rushing across the sky with barely the odd glimpse of the sun or moon showing through to give us hope of an improvement, which never came. I didn't like that at all (I won't say what Hazel thought of it).

The only good thing about it was that the wind was now 60 degrees off the bow and, with just the working jib up, we were doing a bumpy 6 knots most of the time, and in the right direction. With the visibility sometimes down to a quarter of a mile, we sailed into the lee of the island Faial, where it was almost flat calm. Here we took the opportunity to stow the number two genoa, which had been lashed down on deck, and also to tidy up, ready for the short thrash up to Horta in the renewed gale at the unprotected east end of the island.

It appeared that there had been a low sitting over the Azores for several weeks, causing all the bad weather. Together with most of the other crews, we decided that until it improved 'we just ain't going to go'.

It took eight days for the gales to moderate and even then the wind was from the north-east. But oh so gentle. We left. The theory is that when you leave the Azores, you head north until you hit the westerlies and then head for home. A large high over England meant that we would have to get somewhere near Greenland before we got any westerlies.

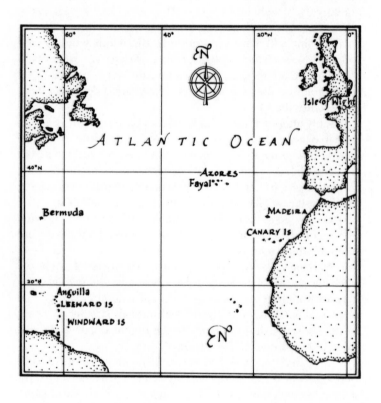

The first four or five days were very pleasant, quiet sailing, close-hauled under full sail on the starboard tack. We soon dropped into that easy rhythm that is so timeless when sailing in reasonable conditions far out in the ocean.

The swallows started to arrive about five days out. The first one flew around for quite a while, before attempting to land, and then made a right mess of it. It tried the spreader, the sail number and finally made it on the guard rail. After a while, and good look round, it got more daring and made several sorties into the cabin. There it took up residence on the starboard pilot berth leecloth. We did our best not to disturb the poor thing.

As night came on, the wind freshened increasingly so that in the early hours we were forced to reef and change down to the working jib. It was quite a game putting on oilskins in those conditions and at the same time not treading on our now rather alarmed guest, who was flapping about all over the place, mostly underfoot. At one time it was seen to be doing a fantastic trapeze act on a long loop of wire from our Walkman, hanging down from a handrail. We got our reef in and the bird seemed quite grateful and sat on Hazel's shoulder. This was all right, until she decided that she just had to go to the loo. Have you ever tried pulling up your knickers while trying not to disturb a swallow sitting on your shoulder? Well, she made it, and the bird was still there.

By morning the wind had eased off again, but as we had suffered a rather disturbed night and the wind was still dead on the nose, we took the easy way out and left the reef and the small jib rigged. After all, we were not racing and the wind might be favourable one day if we waited long enough.

We sailed on all day thus rigged, in a slowly easing breeze. Our friend the swallow left us and soon we were joined by more. Such frail little things, they were about 500 miles from the nearest land. We wondered if they had been blown so far out into the Atlantic by the unseasonal easterlies. Regrettably, not all of them survived. Two of them seemed quite happy for a while and then just keeled over and died. We found it very sad that we could do nothing for them. When you are out there far from land, these little pockets of life take on a deep meaning. You also realise what a small speck of existence you are yourself. One day we will go as the swallow and as soon be forgotten.

By nightfall the wind was down to a gentle breeze, but we were in no mood to make any effort. I was on watch at about 0200. Hazel had done her normal heroic watch from early in the evening to after midnight, letting me catch up on as much sleep as possible. I had been up for quite a while and was about to retire below, to make a leisurely cup of coffee to fight off sleep, when it came to me that it was a rather special kind of a night. It would be a good idea to sit and watch, so as to imprint it upon my memory. The amazing thing about the night was the phosphorescence, the like of which I had never seen in many years of sailing. There was no moon and a thin cover of cloud meant that there were no stars either. However there was light, not only from the normal flashes of phosphorescent fire from our bow wave, and the spasmodic burst from the harmless tumbling of the wavetops, but from an overall inner glow from beneath the sea.

It was as if there were great floodlights switched on down below, sending an eerie glow across the whole surface of the sea. I stood a long time in the hatchway, in a rather soporific daze, gazing out astern in wonder at this magical scene.

The spell was broken by a wave smashing on our weather quarter, followed by another, and yet another, all in the same area. I was not unduly alarmed. It could be dolphins, come to play, attracted by our bow wave. I edged a little higher in my perch.

Dolphins are the most endearing creatures and to watch them playing about your boat must be one of life's greatest simple pleasures. But the breaking, flashing waves were coming closer, straight for us, and appeared to be far too regular. I was now fully awake and more than a little apprehensive. The thought crossed my mind that it could have been a whale. Now I have nothing against whales, in fact I have a great regard for them. But only at a distance, please. This whale, if indeed it was one, was getting far too close. By now I was really alarmed and the adrenalin started to flow. As I said, whales sometimes sink yachts.

I made a move towards the cockpit, still mesmerised by the glow of light, when an extra large crest threw up a great burst of light and lit up the whole scene. To my horror I saw a white yacht with white sails, every detail etched upon my memory in one

flash, bearing straight down on us. Everything went into over-
drive. I jumped for the tiller, frantically disengaged the self-steering
chain, at the same time screamed at the top of my voice for them
to 'look out!' or something equally profound. What I actually said,
I cannot recall. I heaved the tiller to starboard to bear away.

Sherpa Bill responded oh so slowly. I thought for a while she
wasn't going to go, as we were making very little way, but she
did, just.

The other yacht slid by like a ghost, with only feet to spare, not
a soul to be seen, not a light, no sign of life. A phantom in the
night. My panicked cries had brought Hazel from her bunk in an
understandable state of consternation. She quickly summed up
the situation and produced the foghorn, on which she gave
mighty blasts. I, meanwhile, had got hold of our searchlight and
was playing it on the unattended yacht. We had sheered off to a
safe distance and were sailing a parallel course. A head appeared
in the hatchway and I shouted across 'VHF Channel 16!' It took a
while for this to sink in, then the head disappeared and I went
down below to call him up.

He was Dutch. Now I like the Dutch, a lot. In fact, I prefer them
to most, but at this particular moment I was not very fond of this
individual. I think he got my drift. The first thing he did was to put
on his masthead light. At least now we could keep track of where
he was. I then gave him an explosive lecture on the failings and
stupidity of sailors who sail without lights and also my general
feelings about the one that had so nearly run me down in the dark.

I felt a little better after that and calmed down. He told me that
he had left Horta two days before us, and was singlehanded. He
was on his way back to Holland. We bade him goodbye and good
luck and requested that in future he kept his lights burning bright.

The rest of the journey back to Cowes was uneventful. The
wind slowly picked up a bit and freed until, as we came to the
channel, we were on a splendid run in glorious weather.

All stories should finish with a moral, so here goes. Firstly and
upon reflection, I think that perhaps the reason that the swallows
died was that we allowed them down below. No doubt when we
lit our cooking stove, which is the paraffin pressure type, we let
off quite a lot of carbon monoxide fumes. This was probably too

much for the swallows. Remember that in the old days miners too canaries down the mines to warn of dangerous gas.

The second thought, and a request to all you budding Slocums, is please, please use your lights all night, whether or not you are keeping a lookout. The whole art of sailing is to minimise the risks. I recall that Joshua Slocum disappeared at sea. Was he run down in the dark?

With modern charging gear there is no excuse for not show-ing lights. I use an Aquair 50 towing alternator, which I have had for over ten years, and at times I find that I have to leave my lights on during the day to prevent my batteries overcharging. I also use a solar panel and the main motor. With reference to the latter, in case you think that we have to spend hours every day charging, please note that during this cruise of approximately 10,000 miles we used exactly seven gallons of diesel.

Bill Perkes has been sailing for 40 years. He has competed in a three Round Britain races, the AZAB, and five transatlantic races. Altogether he has crossed the Atlantic nine times, twice-singlehanded. Now 'retired', he recently set off to sail around the world in Sherpa Bill, *a 36ft Excalabur class glass fibre sloop.*

Trapped in the ice

by *Mark O'Connell*

I had come to the end: there was nowhere else to go. My boat *Piper* lay motionless in the last patch of ice-free water I could find. Around us, miles of heaving pack-ice. As I turned off the engine and surveyed the incredible scene, I had to admit, despite the danger, that the back-drop to my awful dilemma was ironically beautiful: pure white pack set against the awesome, brooding presence of the vast mountains that make up Kap Farvel, Greenland's southern cape.

I made myself a mug of coffee and sat on deck contemplating how I had come to be here and what exactly would happen next. An EPIRB or HF radio might at least have let someone know where I was, but I had no such luxuries and for the first time I felt truly alone.

I had planned this voyage after returning from a three-year trip to the other end of the world, the Antarctic. There, I had been part of a biological research programme and earned enough money to buy *Piper*. She is a 31ft 6in single chine steel ketch, built in 1965 to a Maurice Griffiths design called Hacathian, a development of the well-known Waterwitch class. With a long central ballast keel and bilge plates, she draws 3ft 8ins and has a 9ft beam. She was moored at Dell Quay in Chichester Harbour during the two years I spent working in hospitals and boat yards while preparing her for the four-month journey to Arctic Greenland.

I sailed north, via the Scilly Isles and Eire. From Cork's wonderful coastline, I crossed the North Atlantic intending to explore Greenland's fjords, sailing as far north as I could during the brief summer months. A band of pack-ice up to 80 miles wide completely encloses Greenland, except for the middle section of the west coast, which becomes relatively ice-free during the summer. It was for this area that I was heading.

The seas around Kap Farvel are notorious for their violent storms, as well as the danger to shipping from ice. My intention, therefore, was to stay well south of it and then head northwards along the west coast, until I could find a passage through the ice to the coast. My plans, however, were drastically altered whilst I was still several hundred miles off the cape. After a brief spell of calm, sunny weather, the skies assumed a rather washy, grey look and I knew something nasty was on the way. Nasty was right and as things deteriorated, I gradually reduced sail until the waves were so vast and the wind speeds so great that all I could do was to run due north under the tiny patch of my storm jib. A true gale in the North Atlantic is something to behold. As we ran before it, every huge roller was breaking and the screeching winds whipped up vast areas of white spray from the surface. The third night of it was the worst: as we surged down each gigantic wave, the rudder was wrenched from my hands and when the sea broke over us I lost control of *Piper* completely. Until she bobbed up again all I could do was grasp the mizzen to prevent being washed from the cockpit. But she came up smiling each time, until the next roller smashed her onto her beam ends yet again. It was a miracle that the masts survived and after being spun around through 180 degrees by one wave I felt pretty lucky, too.

After the storm finally departed, my next concern was to find out where I had been blown to. The sky brightened two days later and my first sun-sight for ten days confirmed what I feared: we were now north of the cape, but on the east coast, *not* the west. I

now had to struggle southwards, round the cape and then continue with my original plan. The storm had added almost a week to my journey. I had a fabulous run to the cape, accompanied by whales and dolphins all the way, until shortly after rounding it, I ran into a major ice problem.

It proved to be a 'bad' ice year, with vast fields of pack remaining in traditionally 'free' areas for much of the summer. I had been sailing northwards, keeping what I thought was well clear of the pack, and I could see its strange glow many miles to the east. When conditions are right, a fog of incredible density is often associated with the ice and it was a bank of this fog that was the start of my problems. When it came down I immediately turned westwards and crawled on under engine only. When the fog lifted the next morning I was surrounded by whiteness. I had sailed into a massive, windblown arm of ice and was now being drawn inevitably towards the main body of the pack. I tried in vain many times to break through the ever-growing barrier, but could find no safe passage, and we were soon completely surrounded.

And so here I was, trapped, with the ice closing in, sitting on the deck of my fine boat, which had already shared many adventures with me. My reverie was violently broken as, suddenly, the ice was on the move again. The sound of creaking, crashing, and grinding as the ice consolidated was like a reverberation from hell itself.

Two huge slabs slammed into *Piper*'s bows while a third piece, travelling at 3 or 4 knots, descended on us from astern. As it hit us, I made feeble, frightened attempts to push it off . . . one man against thousands of tonnes! The davits took the full force of the blow, were bent and then their welds began to rip away from the straining steel deck. They are not modern aluminium tubing, but good old inch-thick steel, and they crumpled like matchwood.

The rudder was thrown to port and I thought it was lost. It was at this moment I could see myself having to climb out onto the ice to die. I really thought 'this is it'. But I wasn't finished yet and, almost without thinking, I fired the engine, kicked her into gear, and opened the throttle to full revs.

By now we were in real danger of being crushed and *Piper*'s bows had ridden up onto the ice. I think this fact, coupled with

the push from the ice astern, caused the ice on the starboard bow to start spinning outwards and away from *Piper*. As it spun, a gap was opened up. I ran to the bows, kicked *Piper* off the port-side ice and leapt back to the cockpit. We were catapulted forward and to my amazement the rudder swung back into place. This was our last chance. I pointed the bows towards the gap and we smashed our way along the ice-channel, bouncing furiously off each side, with the masts shaking so violently I thought they would fall. We shot through to the other side into a newly-opened patch of water and crashed into more ice before I could put her astern. And so we went on: more ice, more batterings, more desperate struggling for open patches of water.

The ice was cold and brutal; millions of tonnes all around us, as deadly as it was beautiful, its sharp acrid smell stinging my nostrils. The next day our fortunes altered when an offshore wind developed and the pack started to spread. My hopes rose. It took two more nightmarish days before *Piper* and I were finally freed. During this time the sea started to heave with the stiffening wind and the vast blocks were thrashing about us chaotically. Once they were in motion, *Piper* was hard pushed to out-run these monsters. The scene was surreal; next time you make a rough-water passage try to imagine the sea filled with enormous blocks of ice waiting to batter at your hull at each turn.

When we finally reached the edge of the pack, I sailed as far away from it as I could safely manage. And then at last, after four continuous days at the helm, I could sleep. I had only had bread and chocolate to eat.

When I look back on it, I remember the intensity of the situation. All I could think of was how I hoped that people would not think I'd wasted my life. I knew the risks and would have died doing what I wanted to do. After all the events that had happened since leaving Dell Quay, I was almost beyond true fear and a strong sense of self-preservation had replaced it.

After a long rest I sailed northwards again and the following week eventually found a way through the ice and into the Fjords. I then followed the comparatively ice-free 'inner-routes' used and marked by the Inuit. The Danish charts I was using showed these routes and proved superior to the British ones. The Arctic pilot for the area has its uses, but is often inaccurate or out of date and must be used with caution at all times.

I spent a succession of glorious weeks exploring the massive fjords and bays and calling in at various Inuit settlements, where I was shown every hospitality. Food, fuel and water can be obtained at most settlements and limited boat repair facilities are available at the larger ones. However, as goods must be imported from Denmark, everything is extremely expensive. 'Wild' meat (seal, etc) can be bought in the settlements, if that is your thing, and fish are abundant and very easy to catch in the fjords.

My journey's end was Greenland's capital Nuuk (Godthåb), where *Piper* was craned out and put in storage under the watchful eye of a Danish boatbuilder I had befriended. Crane facilities are good in the capital and storage fees much the same as they are in this country. However, boats left unattended must be taken out of the water because of winter ice.

Other yachts have visited this wild and magnificent place, although nearly all came across from Canada. Few places in the world offer such excellent sailing, superb anchorages, scenic splendour and a wealth of wildlife. When I return to retrieve *Piper*, I plan to sail further north, but this time with a crew.

Mark O'Connell, aged 30, is currently completing a PhD at Durham University. He has been sailing for six years, normally from Chichester Harbour. Piper, *his steel Hacathian ketch is his first and only boat. As well as his solo voyage to Greenland, he sailed in the Antarctic with two scientific expeditions while working as an assistant biologist for the British Antarctic Survey group*

Maydays in June

by *Dick Durham*

T he tide shrank from the Essex shore and *Almita* ebbed away with it, one jump ahead of the emerging mudflats. We hardened in the sheets bridling the Force 4 and escaped the water's grip to clear the Victorian piles of Southend Pier. The tide carried on and frothily shredded itself round the cast iron posts.

It was June, according to the tide table, but *Almita*'s crew were zipped up in anoraks and polo-neck jerseys. The barrel chest of my burly mate, Rob Livermore, looked even more imposing double-wrapped against the damp and the wind.

Our destination, St Valery Sur Somme, was too long a hard punch in an engineless yacht with the wind dead ahead, so six and a half hours out from Leigh-on-Sea we surged between the piers of Ramsgate harbour and moored up beneath the curiously pink amphi-theatre used to hold this port from toppling into the Downs.

A man in blue, yellow and white oilskins, who was scrubbing a saucepan aboard a small yacht with tinted, slant-eyed 'portholes', asked: 'Did you sail in?'

'Yes.'

'No wonder I didn't hear anything,' he added. 'How will you get out?'

With a tow from you, I thought.

'Same way,' I said.

Our inquisitor had arrived in Ramsgate a week ago from West Mersea. The weather had been too foul all that time for his planned crossing to Calais.

'On my way here I was becalmed,' he said, 'then I found she was filling up. I phoned a Mayday,' he said matter-of-factly. 'I had a helicopter come over.' He seemed rather proud.

Then he discovered his propeller shaft seal – 'doughnut' he called it – had dislodged.

'I simply pushed it back into place and the water stopped coming in. So then I radioed the Coastguard again and told them I was all right.'

But the lifeboat had come out anyway and towed him in.

I nearly choked on my Guinness that night in the Royal Temple Yacht Club when I was told yachts were no longer permitted to enter or leave Ramsgate under sail.

'We have no choice,' I said. 'My boat was built without an engine and has been sailing in and out of harbours for 83 years.'

I was told I was irresponsible. It was 'safer' to have an engine. Then, when I told the gathering of nouveau yachtsmen I had no radio either, that the cabin lamps were oil-fired and that the sole electrics was a car battery for the tricolour, I felt like the man who asked for OK Sauce at the Ritz.

The bronze cannons of the yacht club stood facing out over the Downs, below them the harbour dropped away and I could see the little designer yacht which had both engine and radio, the combination of which had cost the rescue services several thousands of pounds for nothing.

We finished our stout and turned in.

The next morning's north-west Force 6 was mostly cut off from us by Ramsgate. But *Almita's* tall mainsail found enough to blow her out of the harbour. It was still grey and cold and a heavy gybe outside the extended entrance carried away the ensign. The following wind had furled the flag around the boom and when we rocked over, the boom had plucked it from its lashings and dropped it overboard.

A strong tide was running against us as we closed the submerged northern arm of Boulogne harbour. We could not weather it and Rob wound up the centre-plate and I held my breath as we shot over the top of the digue nord.

As we came in line with the dolphin marking the end, I said 'If we're going to hit it, we'll soon know.' We didn't. We put in a board to clear an outgoing P&O Ferry and soon after were moored alongside the miserable pontoons allowed a few square feet of brackish water in among the fishing boats.

As Rob heaved off his oilskins and plunged into his dunny bag for a phrase book, a handsome young couple beckoned to me from a little 20ft cruiser on the next pontoon.

'I see you have a courtesy flag,' said a lanky young fellow with a stoop I imagined he had cultivated in order to be able to stow himself below, 'But you've no ensign.'

I told him what had happened and he ordered a glamorous wife to bring up a tot of whisky each for Rob and me. Before we could take a sip he said, 'Stop. It's sunset. Don't touch a drop yet.' He rose and unclipped his nylon ensign from the backstay. 'We like to get it right,' he said gravely.

Just minutes later we were tucked under a blue and white squared tablecloth deciphering the fish on the menu.

Rob, with a cigarette hanging from his mouth, consulted his phrase book, but failing to find the requisite words halted the busy waiter with 'Got a light mate?' at which the fellow simply placed his Cricket on the table and moved on with his orders.

'I can put this away then,' said Rob.

When our bowls of orange fish soup arrived he was able to utilise the phrase book after all – under the shortest leg of the table to prevent further spillage.

'I know one thing,' said my crew after his soup, *raie avec poivre* and cheese, "if I lived here, I'd be about fifteen stone."

Next morning grey drizzling low cloud swallowed up the high rise blocks of flats opposite our berth. Rob's burnt, sleepy face broke open only to demand tea and enquire, 'Your show's on in a minute, isn't it?'

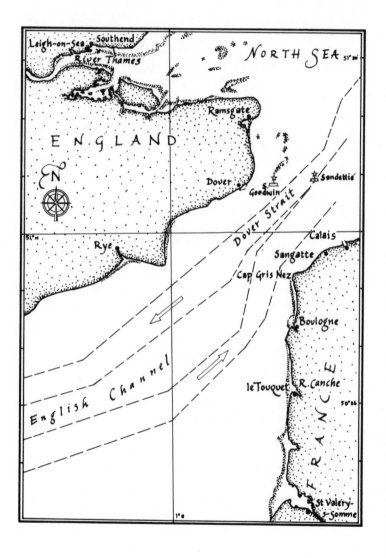

Rob is more at home stiffening wobbly buildings in the calipers of scaffolding than at sea. But his demanding job has given him a physique which can tear an anchor from the sea-bed against a gale and a spring flood and a sardonic attitude toward abstract predictions such as the shipping forecast.

The predictions included fog and a south-west Force 5 for Dover, Wight, so I too returned to my bunk.

The inclement weather gave my crew a whole week in which to practice his French on the fisherfolk of Boulogne. But the next night, as we sipped vin rouge in the Hotel Hamiot, Rob's ponderous request for another round was overheard by a bearded skeleton who spoke English – who *was* English and spoke reasonable French.

The skeleton turned out to be one Nick Paton. His yellow pallor and shrunken head made brown pools of his hollow eyes. His trousers hung off him like wind-socks - they weren't baggy but his legs were so thin that they did not interfere in the least with their cut. He joined us and drank with us and we all drank too much because now we had a translator.

Nick coughed a lot and had fits of the shudders. He told us he imported cars from Belgium to Gibraltar and regularly based himself in Boulogne, because it was cheap and he had friends at the Hotel Hamiot. But the dampness and the regular fogs did not agree with him, he said.

The fogs did not agree with us, either, as we stewed in the harbour, wishing for clear skies. The River Canche had been one destination on route. Instead, Nick drove us there on a day trip in a Saab estate he was awaiting a buyer for.

Nick ate virtually nothing and drank a lot of *pastis*. We all did, adopting the Hotel Hamiot as our second home. We would walk away in the early hours of the morning as the night porter wiped down the large plate glass windows, scraping condensation into a bucket. Then we would arrive through the fog for breakfast the following day.

One night, five huge men burst into the bar. Two went behind the counter and poured themselves beer. The others disappeared in the kitchen, returning with French loaves stuffed with cheese, ham and gherkins. The bar tender grinned obsequiously at the biggest of the men, who wore a large gun on his waist.

Nick whispered 'Police . . . they come in most nights, but usually later. It's their bar.'

The big cop looked like Alain Delon and wore a red cravat which he kept adjusting. This required using a large wall mirror advertising beer. His cravat provided him a regular opportunity to gaze at his lean face.

He drank a lot of wine and did not bat an eyelid when Rob asked to have a look at his gun. He pulled it out – an exercise of some duration owing to the length of the thing. It was a Magnum, I was told. When Rob handed the huge piece of personal ordnance back to the cop, he left it on the bar for the rest of the evening. The following night he brought in his trophies to show us. He was a crackshot, apparently.

Sunday's thick fog made the town seem as though it had closed forever. The young couple on the small yacht were preparing to leave.

'You're not going out in this, are you?' I asked, and told them the local met readings gave visibility down to 50 metres at the Sandettie and there was no reason to suppose it was any better further south – they planned a return to the yacht's berth at Rye.

'We've both got jobs to go back to, so fog or no fog we go,' said the humpy-backed husband. His pretty young wife, who appeared to have come through a beauty salon on the way from cabin to cockpit, added, 'We get a bit braver every time we come over.'

The husband said 'We had one Bermudan registered ship who nearly took us out. Hadn't seen us. But they must be so tired by the time they get here.'

I watched them dissolve in the fog and thought about the skipper's last remark. Surely he did not believe a ship's crew cast off and remained at the helm till they reached the other side of the world? No, he must have meant something else, I pondered. Then I remembered him lowering his ensign after sunset. I offered up a small prayer.

A day after the little yacht's departure we thankfully got some slightly clearer weather. With the last of the north running tide we set off. We would not get any further south within the confines of

our vacance and planned at least to hop round to Calais and cross the Channel from there.

The ailing Mr Paton had shipped aboard, desperate to see some sunshine and get away from the damp, tart aroma of Boulogne. The fog hemmed in a cocktail of crushed crabs' legs and decapitated cod, staring incredulously from the cobbles of the fish quay.

Almita was squeezed to loo'ard by the Sealink ferry *Hengist*, as she sailed out. I knew her master would be praying the little green yacht with the red sails did not put in a board suddenly across his bows. He must have known we were running out of water, but we let the sheets fly and rubbed against the barnacle-calloused piles of the harbour. As the *Hengist* passed she gave a long, low groan of thanks. A crewman came out on the stern deck and, gazing down at us, beat his chest with his fist to signify what the captain's heart had been doing. Then he smiled and gave us a thumbs up. It had cost us a little top coat, but nothing else.

A fair, light wind ghosted us through the fog, which shut in yet again as soon as we had cleared the outer harbour. The mist cut off the coast of France and we had little to give us any sense of speed, except the lobster pots, which flared up out of the gloom, their flags wrenched horizontal by the fierce tug of the tide. They passed us like telegraph poles from a train. At one time the fog lifted to reveal an awesome Mount Everest towering over us. Cap Gris Nez was a bit close. I had overreacted to the sound of fog-horns in the Channel.

An old course line in pencil across the chart, from Cap Gris Nez to the South Goodwin light vessel, now uncannily appeared to mark the way the heavens had been dissected. For we sailed from the damp murk into dazzling sunshine, as though across a threshold. As the bowsprit probed the new welcome warmth, the dinghy was still lost in haze.

When the tide came against us, we heaved the fisherman over the side and lay in the glassy swell off Cap Gris Nez. Nick and I rowed ashore to Sangatte for water, cheese, a jar of fish soup and beer. Back aboard, I left the crew to picnic, whilst I bathed in the strong tide with a long bowline round my waist.

Nick's short sea passage had invigorated him. He was eating

Maydays in June

everything he could lay hands on, his face filled out, the ghastly yellow pallor turned to bronze, so it was a pity to spoil it, as we did, by mooring in the outer harbour in Calais. The heatwave which had brought Nick back to life also encouraged chemical frenzy in the horribly polluted water. Noxious gases rose from the purple-coloured surface water, glazing over the gunmetal fittings on *Almita*'s deck.

The only way we could bear to sleep in such appalling odour was to take hearty slugs of *pastis*. The smell of aniseed killed the stench of the harbour.

Two nights of that and Nick decided to return to Boulogne. I rowed him ashore and we walked round the yacht canal. There we spotted a little boat which seemed familiar. A limp nylon ensign hung off the backstay. A pretty woman coloured her face in a mirror on deck. A humpy-backed lean man pored over the pages of an almanac.

It was the little boat we'd seen in Boulogne.

The owner caught my eye.

'Hello,' he said, 'we've taken an extra week's hols. Can't miss a heatwave like this.'

Later that night in the Calais Yacht Club, the young skipper told me over a beer he'd had engine failure in the fog. The throbbing of what seemed like a nearby ship had caused him to lose his nerve.

'We had to send out a Mayday call. There was no wind, what else could I do?' he implored despairingly.

A pilot launch had picked them up and towed them into the ferry port.

The young fellow slugged another mouthful of Stella. He had lost his confidence. Sailing was suddenly something alien to him.

Then, sensing my silence, he said quickly, 'It was such a pity there was no wind. I've had her up to 14 knots with the kite up.'

Dick Durham, a journalist on the Daily Star, contributes regularly to Yachting Monthly. He has also written a book, On and Offshore, *about his adventures with* Almita, *his engineless 26ft centreboard cutter.*

We're not out of the woods yet

by *Kathy Webb*

Cape Horn was behind us, but we were not out of the woods yet. The 2,000 mile passage from the Beagle Channel north to Montevideo was to prove the most arduous Alan, Portia, our sixteen-year-old daughter, and I had undertaken aboard our 45ft steel cutter *Supertramp*.

The first and worst obstacle was Le Maire Strait. We kept scaring ourselves with the pilot book's warnings of the dangers of the tidal overfalls and 8-10 knot currents. No wonder the old sailing ship masters feared it more than Cape Horn. At the turn of the century, many ships were wrecked each year in the narrow, mountain-lined gateway which links the Atlantic and Pacific Oceans, squeezing the mighty tidal waters between Tierra del Fuego and Staten Island.

The pilot warns to attempt it only with a fair wind and tide - a contrary wind makes the already dangerous overfalls so unmanageable they can overwhelm a big ship, let alone an underpowered sailing vessel like ours. To predict the wind more than six hours ahead is impossible in this winter region of storms, so

We're not out of the woods yet

you can imagine our dismay when the Captain of Puerto Williams, the Chilean naval base in the Beagle Channel, told us that for political reasons his opposite number in Ushaia, on the Argentine side, had refused to allow us to wait for favourable weather in Puerto Espanol, the closest anchorage to the strait. Instead, we had to settle for Isla Picton, 60 miles west in Chilean waters – a 10 to 12-hour journey from our destination.

After three days of incessant gales, we departed Caleta Banner, Isla Picton, at 2115 on Saturday 24 August, while the southwesterly was still blowing 18 knots and the barometer was high, hoping to get through Le Maire in the short-lived calm period that often occurs between the westerly depressions. The seas were bumpy in the Beagle Channel, and outside the cover of Isla Nueva we felt the awesome force of the South Pacific swell on our starboard beam. As we sailed by, the Chilean radio lookout on Isla Nueva called to wish us good luck. We were going to need it. Ten minutes earlier, our self-steering rudder had snapped. We were going to have to hand-steer all the way to Uruguay in the cold, storm-swept South Atlantic winter.

Picking up the lights on the Isla Grande de Tierra del Fuego, we made good time through the night for our appointment with slack water at the entrance to Le Maire Strait. Occasionally the breeze puffed from the north-east but we thought it was a fluke, since we hadn't seen a northeasterly since we were in the Magellan Straits two months earlier... fate couldn't be so cruel as to give us the one wind we dreaded for this perilous passage!

By 0500 we were out past the Cabo Buen Suceso light, on the east shore of the strait, and angled across to position ourselves in the middle of the 20-mile wide channel, clear of the dangerous tidal overfalls on both sides. Now, as the tide began to flood, the fickle wind chose its moment to blow strongly from the north-east. Fear gripped our hearts. There was no going back. We were trapped in this sluice gate between the Atlantic and Pacific Oceans, with a 5-knot tide on our tail and a contrary 35-knot head wind.

The waves began to stand up in unnatural pyramid shapes, bubbling and boiling on the same spot so *Supertramp* was in a quandary about how to deal with them. Although giving the illusion of moving forward, she was actually tossed and rolled without making any headway. Dawn revealed the south-west corner of Tierra del Fuego, blue with white snow-capped mountains. In the half-light, Staten Island appeared a sombre, uniform grey.

Unable to tack across the strait because we had to avoid the overfalls off Cabo St Diego to the west and Staten Island to the east, we furled the sails and motored at full throttle. There followed seven of the longest hours of our lives, when what should have been a two-hour romp through the 20-mile strait, with a favourable wind and tide, became a battle for survival as we crashed into the huge overfalls, water swamping the whole boat and the bitter north-east wind chilling us so our teeth chattered and we shook with the cold.

We had to make it through in the six hours before the tide turned against us, but our position against the land had hardly altered after two hours of slogging it out. Steering was critical as the whirlpools and tidal overfalls sent us wallowing one way and stumbling the other, always on the point of being knocked down and overwhelmed by the great perpendicular seas. Ironically, the wind-torn strait was alive with gleaming black and white arctic dolphins, leaping joyfully along beside us through the terrible overfalls. At one with their element, they were oblivious to our plight.

We struggled until we could see the second promontory on Staten Island and then gradually Cabo St Diego, the notorious north-west sentinel. The pilot advises ships to give Cabo St Diego at least a 10-mile berth, but that wasn't enough. Suddenly, we were in a maelstrom of jumping, smacking, colliding overfalls. 'Christ, take a look at that lot,' Alan shouted, as he swung the bow north-east, angling even further away from the point to get us out of danger.

Slowly, the north side of Staten Island began to open up, stretching away 50 long miles to the east. Five freezing, wet, nerve-wracking hours later we were through the Strait but still had to contend with the wind, which veered northwesterly and increased to gale force. We had to get some distance between ourselves and Le Maire Strait, as it was still a threat. If the gale became too strong to beat into, we couldn't heave to so close to Staten Island, for its north coast would be a lee shore. And if we didn't sail well clear we could be sucked back in by the tide when it turned, strengthened by the northwesterly gale. Another factor was that if we were forced to run before the storm, our only course would be back around Cape Horn.

With all this in mind, we pounded into the ugly grey seas for another four hours, until we were 25 miles north of Cabo St Diego and 15 miles north of Staten Island; then, exhausted and drenched, we hove to and monitored our position on the satellite navigator. During the night the waves began to smash *Supertramp* so thunderously that we feared we were drifting too close to the eastern end of Staten Island, where the overfalls are so treacherous that ships are warned 'under no circumstances to approach within 15 miles'. But a sat-nav fix showed us to be moving northeast with the current out of danger, so we took no action.

Next morning, Staten Island was astern, its sharp snow peaks clear against the sky, and we were never more grateful to see the back of anything. Our drift eastwards continued, but it was late afternoon before the gale subsided enough for us to get underway.

In the freezing wind and spray it was impossible to steer for more than an hour at a time, which meant a rigorous timetable of one hour on, two hours off, 24 hours a day for the three of us. What with sail changes, navigation, cooking and general chores, we seldom got more than an hour's sleep in between watches and often none at all. If it was gruelling for Alan and me, both fit and healthy, it was an amazing feat of courage by Portia, still weak from the hepatitis she'd suffered in the Chilean Channels.

Hand-steering alone at night in the Southern Ocean is a traumatic experience at any age, but for a 16-year-old girl to wrestle the heavy helm as the wind howls and the great seas roar and miss menacingly in the pitch darkness, crashing aboard with relentless regularity - only a lifeline and a desperate grip on the wheel preventing her being swept overboard - it was a terrifying ordeal.

The northwesterly gales prevailed all the way to Montevideo and we were alternately forced east, when the wind and seas decreased enough for us to beat into them, or hove to under storm

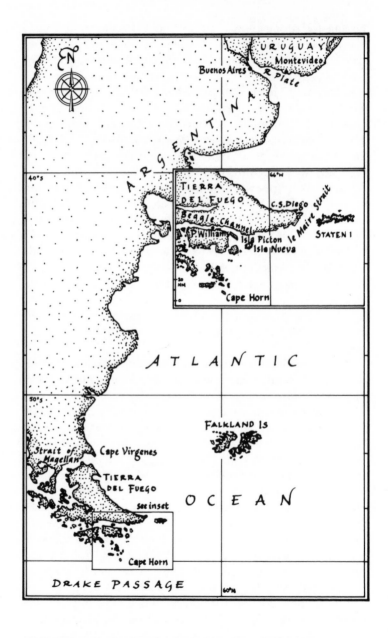

jib when they reached their peak. Usually we held our ground, but one night we lost 20 miles to the south lying ahull 150 miles east of the Strait of Magellan, probably an effect of the massive tides at Cape Virgenes, the eastern entrance. Our intention was to take advantage of the calmer seas in the lee of the Argentine coast, but instead we were driven 300 miles east, out to the Falkland Islands. My log for 30 August read:

'Anxious and uneasy all afternoon and evening as the gale goes on unmercifully and the barometer keeps falling - it's like we'll never get out of these 50-55 degree south latitudes. We are worried about the proximity of the Falklands to the east should the storm last much longer, because lying ahull we are being driven that way.'

After an awful night of black squalls, sleet and hailstones, around 0500 the depression turned southwesterly; almost too strong to utilise, but we couldn't afford to squander the only free wind since the Beagle Channel and our chance to escape from a lee shore. We hoisted the storm jib and fled before it. By 1500 we had thankfully cleared the north-west tip of West Falkland Island by 30 miles. Shortly afterwards, as night fell, squall followed vicious squall, the wind direction switching to south, then back to south-west, and increasing in velocity until only Alan had the strength to steer. Doggedly, he braved the blasting hailstones and sleet, determined to hang on to the storm jib as long as possible to get out of the trouble spot. The hailstones were three inches deep over the cockpit and decks after one sustained horizontal 70-knot hail squall, with great black clouds and the sea smoking with wind-driven spray. It was impossible to turn and face it without being blinded. Just before midnight the wind increased without warning to hurricane force and we tore down the sail doing 10 knots and carried on at 6 under bare poles, flying over the peaks on the verge of broaching. For the first time ever, we prepared to trail warps to slow *Supertramp*, but instead tried rounding up and lying ahull and found she was riding the huge waves like a duck, although the motion was radical.

From my log:

'2400 hours: now the wind is howling at hurricane force and the waves roaring and breaking and seething, the gale raging on

and on, the squalls bouncing hailstones on the deck like machine gun fire, alternating with freezing sleet. It's a frightening place this South Atlantic, we'll all be glad when we're out of it. This is one of the worst gales we've experienced. The wind sounds like a maddened animal and the waves fling us sideways as they hit with terrifying force. Nights like this we are so glad of a good strong steel boat that will do everything we ask of her - run before a Force 11 gale, or lie ahull and lift as the monster waves rush up, leaving them thwarted, roaring harmlessly under the keel.

'I have seized the break from steering to cook the last two legs of lamb from the whole sheep presented to us by the Chilean Navy on Isla Picton - they are crackling in the oven with the door tied to restrain them and we are grateful for the homely Sunday dinner smell, which lends the stormy night a determined air of domesticity, like there's really going to be a tomorrow. Our nightly stew has become an institution on this voyage, where conditions and fatigue demand cooking be kept at the minimum; to a mixture of fresh carrots, celery, chick peas, lentils, ears of green wheat and rice, we add the roast lamb for Alan and me, and canned chicken or tuna for Portia, whose hepatitis diet doesn't allow mutton.'

On 1 September we thankfully crossed over the latitude of 50 degrees south, leaving the worst area of storms behind us. Although from Le Maire Strait we had only logged 300 miles, they were the hardest we have ever sailed.

One day, a ship that at first looked like a floating container turned out to be a Russian scientific motor fishing vessel. We called them on the VHF. There was a delay while the officer on watch found a sailor to translate for him in halting, formal English. The concept of the freedom to own your own boat and travel the world seemed too strange for them to comprehend, but they offered to help us in any way possible and sounded very sincere in their friendliness.

Now, in between the gales, there were spells of good sailing and even periods of calm.

Log: Tuesday 2 September;

'A beautiful day, blue skies, sunshine and thousands of albatross circling and wheeling above the bright water. For the first time in six months we opened the hatches and let the fresh air dry out

some of the dampness and mildew. The barometer is high and steady and the wind gentle from the north-west as we beat under single-reefed mainsail and genoa. It is still cold enough for us to be rugged up, but there is a promise in the warmth of the sun of better days to come. During Portia's watch, a school of killer whales raced on the bow for a while, recognisable by their piebald colouring and large triangular fins. The small penguins, which we have seen by day and heard by night honking to each other since Tierra del Fuego, were out in great numbers undulating at speed, their silky bodies flashing black and white against the blue ocean. Encouraged by the fine weather, I braved a strip wash, the first since Isla Picton, and not to be outdone, Alan and Portia followed suit. Now we all smell beautiful.'

On Saturday 7 October we passed out of the Roaring Forties into the variables, blasting through the night like an arrow, arms aching with the effort of steering under full sail in the brisk northerly winds. Although leaving 40 degrees latitude behind was another obstacle overcome, King Neptune was not done with us yet. We were now approaching the region of the notorious *pamperos*, the violent squalls from the Argentine pampas which plague the sailor along this coast. The warning signs are northerlies for a day or so, veering to north-east and becoming gusty with a slowly falling barometer - a lull then a cold front from the south-west, heralded by a huge sausage-shaped roll of cumulus cloud.

True to form, the glass started to drop and that afternoon the wind veered north-east and increased. We shortened sail, wishing we'd never read about the damned sausage cloud. Every way we looked there was another one on the horizon. Halfway through preparing the evening meal Alan decided to drop the mainsail. It was now blowing a full gale and the seas were big and unruly. Hove to under storm jib only, we had another go at dinner, but then the lightning started, illuminating the black night like daylight - jagged fork lightning zig-zagging down to the sea in burning white hot lines, sometimes in sets of four or six forks, while blindingly brilliant sheet lightning was flashing simultaneously all around the horizon. We had never before witnessed such an explosion of violent electrical forces and awful power and energy.

We're not out of the woods yet

To add to our uneasiness, for the first time ever, we beheld the unnerving spectacle of St Elmo's Fire, illuminating the masthead so it glowed with an unearthly green light - no wonder the old sailors thought it was a ghostly omen of doom. By the light of the flashes we were searching for the dreaded sausage cloud and suddenly there it was, bearing down on us. Squalls had been hitting us from every direction, but the one that accompanied the cloud was so strong that the high-pitched whine of the wind sounded like someone was strangling it. We doused the storm jib at the double, leaving the *pampero* nothing to destroy, and then came the rain in torrents. We were glad to lie ahull, watching the lightning through the cabin windows as we finished our dinner and coffee by the paraffin lamp, laughing uproariously at Alan's mimicry of peg-legged Captain Ahab from Melville's *Moby Dick*, pointing a bony finger aloft, eyes crazed with fear as he recognised his own doom in St Elmo's Fire playing around the masthead.

The next day we approached the 120 mile-long estuary that forms the River Plate, on the north shore of which lies Montevideo, the capital city of Uruguay, while Buenos Aires, the first city of Argentina, graces the southern side. Both cities must be approached through dredged channels as the maximum depth in the river is 33ft, which means a wicked sea can rise very easily. The chart was littered with wrecks that had either run on to the numerous unmarked banks, or been broken up on the shallow bottom in storms. Most of them are hazards to navigation and present a dismal sight, lit by a solitary flashing light, spars and funnels rising above the waves. The prevailing northwesterly winds have a strange effect on the tides and current, making the river even more dangerous by reducing the water levels to less than those charted; and bad visibility compounds the navigator's problems.

Nobody got much sleep as the wind increased and faded and veered, and we reefed the mainsail and reduced the headsail, then shook out the reef, then put it back in again. Until we were past the notorious 16 mile-long Banco Ingles at the southern entrance, everyone was up and alert. That behind us, we could afford to relax more. The waves in the shallow water of the River Plate had peaks so brilliant with phosphorescence that the scene looked almost too melodramatic, like an animated Victorian stage set - rolling crests flashing silver-white against black water and sky, and lightning illuminating the darkness and reflecting in jagged red lines in the compass bowl.

A vessel appeared suddenly on my port beam through the driving rain, close enough for me to see three lights. Before I could recover from the shock, it had swept by at amazing speed and disappeared into the darkness, like a ghost ship. As we crossed deeper into the estuary, the seas flattened out until it was like a lake. In the dawn light the Praticos Recalada Lightship, where the merchant vessels pick up their pilots to guide them through the dredged channels, appeared on the bow. A Dutch freighter overtook us. 'Steer a direct course,' the Officer on watch advised cheerfully. 'There are no obstacles to navigation between here and Montevideo.'

The water was now a muddy brown and green colour and we could see four ships at a time smudged against the dull horizon. Montevideo appeared on the skyline, the tall grey skyscrapers and cathedrals merging with the mist. A new land to discover, a safe port at the end of an arduous voyage and a joyous release from the fear and tensions of the Southern Ocean.

Crowded happily in the cockpit, we asked ourselves if we would ever go back to the Southern Ocean. Portia answered 'Never.' Alan countered, 'Without doubt.' And I said, 'Well, not for a long time, anyway.'

Kathy Webb has done thousands of miles of long distance cruising aboard Supertramp, *a 45ft steel cutter, with husband Alan and daughter Portia.*

Atlantic birthday treat

by *John Stevens*

My mid-Atlantic birthday was celebrated by brilliant blue skies and sparkling sea. Around mid-morning it became unmistakably apparent that a disproportionate amount of sea was sparkling on the inside of the boat, as well as the outside. Two manual pumps being worked with feverish zeal failed to stay ahead of the game. For a time, it looked as if we might be taking to the life-raft in ideal conditions with about 600 miles to go to reach the nearest land.

Between Bermuda and the Azores, and up to our present position, we had seen, perhaps, six ships and one aircraft, so it could have been a long paddle. It looked like the prelude to my first cry for help in over 30 years of ocean racing.

The leak was fairly obviously from a skin fitting, but there was so much water sloshing about that we couldn't find the source and our beautiful Swan 44 was settling comfortably. It looked to me like twenty minutes to stepping off time, when I felt we should abandon the search for the leak. I put the boat on the other tack to give us a chance of lifting the guilty pipe out of the water.

Fortunately, the idea worked and water stopped flooding in. We pumped the surplus tons back into the Atlantic and set about finding the problem.

What appeared to have happened was that water was syphoning back through a massive electric bilge pump that we had fitted in America as a safety measure. It seems that the pump would sense water, fill its large pipes with sea water, then, having primed its syphon, the pump stopped and water came in much quicker than we could pump it out.

This was a high point of drama in our 3,000 miles from Bermuda to Cowes, but we had our other moments with gales, whales and a few more gales.

In fact, we left gentle Bermuda, where we had fitted into the life-style with slothful ease, and sailed straight into a gale which lasted on and off for the first five days. Day five, particularly, gave us squalls of up to 50 knots which dampened and depressed the gallant crew.

Dick Hedger, the skipper and owner, navigated us to our landfalls in the Azores, Ushant and Portland Bill, in a fog, with marvellous patience and accuracy. More importantly, he brought along his two charming daughters, Kate and Louise. Both accomplished sailors, they were so pretty and cheerful that no depression seemed to last too long. They are the only people I know who look slim and *soigné* in oilskins.

On both legs we had John Bibby, who recently campaigned the half-tonner, *Insatiable*. His brother, Will, joined us from the Azores to England. The crew from Bermuda to the Azores was much strengthened by Nick Taylor, a journalist from Georgia. He had the job of calling me from my sleep at two in the morning in heavy rain and gale. He tapped my shoulder and announced, 'There's a film on the afterdeck . . . it's called Four Hours to Dawn . . . and you're invited.'

During one of the heavy blows, the stitching on the genoa foot began to unravel and we found that we had loaned out our sailmaker's needles in Bermuda and not recovered them. We had the ghastly job of repairing the roller-reefed genoa on the heaving foredeck under torrential spray with a housewife's ordinary round needle and a pair of pliers. It took over three hours of hard

Atlantic birthday treat

work. Never be without sailmaker's needles.

It wasn't all hard work, we made the 1,800 miles from Bermuda to Faial in 12 days. At least three days were with southwesterlies blowing 35 knots – fast downhill sailing in bright sunshine. But before we made our landfall the wind came round on to the nose and it rained buckets. Actually, the northeasterlies that began then blew for our five days in the Azores and dogged us all the way home.

The Azores must be one of the world's great landfalls. The island of Pico, just beside Horta harbour in Faial, is, quite simply, the highest mountain in Portugal. It rises straight out of the sea to 7,000ft and its top is covered in snow, even in early summer when we were there.

You can actually see Pico from 97 miles away. We didn't, because it was raining heavily, but we certainly saw that lovely mountain from over 30 miles away.

We came into Horta harbour late in the evening from a northerly gale that had our windspeed indicator locked on its stop at 60 miles an hour. You will readily understand how grateful we were to be in the warm flat water of the Azores.

Everyone was so kind to us there. We arrived at about 2230 and Horta (about half the size of Penzance) was closing up. So we asked at the rococo police station for a restaurant that might be open. We were given directions and we pushed off into the night. After a minute or two we heard running feet and the policeman caught up with us. He had seen we were tired so he came to take us to the restaurant to make sure we didn't miss our way.

The Azores is like an idealised England 200 years ago. The people are kind and so untouched by tourism that acquisitiveness is simply not part of their nature. When you leave what they call 'the City' and drive your hire car through the villages, people turn out to wave because they get so few visitors. It is difficult to spend much more than two pounds on a pleasant meal and excellent local wine and a black coffee and a big glass of local brandy is less than 40p.

The islands get so much Atlantic rain that they are as green as England, but bananas, figs, oranges and lemons grow in beautifully ordered groves. It is not usually quite as hot as the

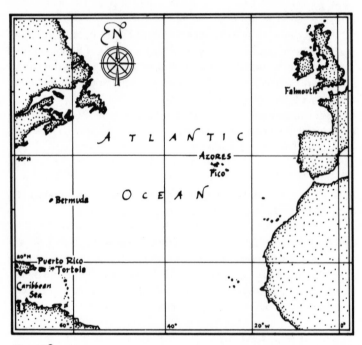

Townsend

Mediterranean, but it is warm and comfortable.

The Azores are very cut off and the people tend to do what their grandfathers did. It's not legal, but in the remote villages there is a notable tendency to produce a wonderful moonshine brandy. I made friends with a delightful Azorean who had spent years in America and he was kind enough to give me a bottle – like the very best grappa.

Azoreans, up till now, have lived by whaling and there are probably as many Azoreans in Nantucket as there are on the island of Faial. Certainly there are more Azoreans in America and elsewhere than there now are in all the Azores. When Portugal joined the EEC, whaling became illegal and the 1,600 people employed directly in whaling were put out of work. No one applauds whaling but, these generations of oarsmen – they row to catch their whales – helmsmen and harpooners will have to look to tourism to make a living.

The Azores have much to offer tourists who value peace and quiet. More than that, they have some of the best game fishing in the world just a mile or two from Horta Harbour. I hope tourism is successful for them: but not too quickly.

All these lovely islands are steep and volcanic. Indeed, Faial had a volcanic eruption in 1957 (only yesterday in geological terms) that added about a fifth to the existing island, incinerated its lighthouse and buried two villages. The old lighthouse, in 1956 conscientiously throwing it powerful beam out to the west, now had a new landmass all around it and a huge peak in front of its former view, rising to well over 1,000ft and smelling like a million coke fires.

When we left the Azores, we added our name and logo to the celebrated paintings on Horta harbour's walls – '*Flourish*, Swan 44, New York to Cowes 1989 '.

Any yachtsman who has stopped off at the Azores will know the kind of intelligent help we were generously given by Peter in his famous Café Sport. It was Peter who rang Bob Silverman for me. A first-rate sailor who repaired our damaged genoa and checked all our sails over, Bob is also the author of an excellent yachtsman's guide to the islands. Peter's particular skill has been not merely to attract the visiting yachtsmen, but to retain the full custom of the local Azorean sailors. For their part, the Azorean seamen look very kindly on the international yachtsmen. They clearly feel that anyone who has got there at all has earned his yellow wellies!

A major drama confronted the three-man crew of *Doublejay* when a killer whale struck their concrete boat as they approached Horta. Fortunately, their yacht was pitching heavily so the punched hole, about a foot across, was mostly above the water-line. Even so, they were confronted by quite severe flooding problems in the heavy seas. They didn't see the killer whale, but there was considerable noise on impact and they found fragments of blood and black blubber round the hole.

We saw few ships in the broad Atlantic – one freighter, bound from Canada to Brazil, and a distant tanker – but it is in the way of things at sea that we actually had to alter course to avoid the third vessel we saw, in the night. Our lights were shining brightly and we gave them a brief stroboscopic display as well, but on she came. We were running and our preventers made it awkward to alter for him and we were showing our red to his starboard bow. We tucked rather close around his stern and when we called him up on Channel 16 there was no response. It was a very large freighter and I don't suppose anyone made themselves aware that we were there at all. So few ships, such a big ocean and we would actually have hit the blasted thing. It seemed incredible.

Also incredible was the skill we developed in locking the wheel when we were close-hauled (which we were for most of the time on the second leg, with sustained northeasterlies). On at least one occasion, the boat steered herself for well over 24 hours, indeed until we had to change course.

The sea temperature was noticeably warmer on the Bermuda-Azores section and contained much more of interest, below, or above. For example, we saw shearwaters and petrels all the way, even 1,000 miles from land. From time to time we saw shy, giant turtles solemnly making their way across the ocean. The colour of pale copper, these dignified creatures would up-end and dive if we showed the slightest undue interest.

Whales we found by nearly running into them, twice. The first time I was steering and the whale was right across our path and

absolutely under the bow. I assumed he was asleep, but he reacted a good deal more quickly than I did by sinking and turning. Anyway, I didn't feel us touch him. The second time Will Bibby, quicker than I was, steered round him.

On another occasion, two whales surfaced alongside and both were much bigger than our 44ft. They gave a lengthy snuffle from their vent holes and went their gentle way.

The dolphin show was staged for us about every other day and sometimes at night. The night shows were best, illuminated as they were, by brilliant phosphorescence. Up to twenty dolphins would tuck themselves under and around the bow, their perfect round bodies making a long tube of vivid blue light which strongly lit our bow and traced their lovely movements a long time after they had passed. Four stars of the show would race off into the black night. Minutes later you would see four blue streaks racing at 30 knots or more for the bow.

You would be sure they would destroy themselves on our sharp stem, when at the last split second, in a flurry of blue light, they would reverse their flight and rejoin the team, leaping and dancing in the night.

In the day, you could be more sure it was a show. If you lay on the starboard side of the bow, that's where the show was. If you moved to the port side, that's where the troop performed. The dolphins, too, would roll on their sides and look straight at you with their knowing eyes. When they got really excited they would call out among themselves, like sophisticated birds.

Nearer home, in the colder Atlantic, there were fewer crea-tures, and we had to make do with the odd shark. Very few birds flew in the northerly Atlantic, until the seagulls of Brittany told us we were really near home.

Landfall in pitch dark on Ushant was magic, because of the scents. After a month at sea, my sense of smell was incredibly acute and my breathing very clear. I'm told I snore, which is probably a dreadful calumny because I've never heard it myself, but I wasn't snoring at the end of this trip.

At first, the blessed landfall light of Ushant was surrounded by the heavy, honey perfume of Brittany's gorse. As we came within ten miles of Brest, as I live and breathe we could smell the

Atlantic birthday treat

Gauloises – all the glorious French scents of a civilised city. Later, as we moved along and before we moved away into the broader wastes of the English Channel, I could smell the fecund intensity of earth – mother earth, and we were nearly home.

Bang on the nose again, the disappointing northeasterlies compelled us to raise the lights of Les Hanois close to, before diverting to miss the Casquets. Our landfall was in fog a mile and a bit off St Albans Head. We could see people walking on the cliffs in England's historic heat wave. It was quite cold down where we were, bouncing up and down in our oilskins.

When we entered the Solent, I was so depressed at the notion of getting the train back to London that I went below and read a book. But when we turned into Cowes harbour on Monday evening, all our wives were jumping up and down like marionettes on the Island Sailing Club pontoon. My Cynthia had been there since early morning, to be sure that the crew coming out of the Atlantic would get a warm welcome. It was one of the happiest moments of my life.

John Stevens, a Public Relation Consultant, has been sailing for 45 years. He currently sails from the Hamble in an Oyster 41, but in a lifetime of yachting has crewed in boats of all shapes and sizes, from 30ft to 100ft, including sailing to Spain in a replica of Slocum's Spray.

Wrongful arrest

by *Alan Bond*

'Lunch is ready.' Johanna's voice called up from the galley. I took a look around. It was a perfect day, the sort usually confined to brochures at boat shows.

We were four miles off Charlotte Head, with Cape Hawke sparkling in the sunshine on the starboard quarter and Sugar Loaf Point, crowned by its light, fine on the starboard bow. Seal Rocks, beneath the point, extend out to sea for several miles. Very nasty, but the course we were on would clear the most seaward of them by a good two miles.

A final glance to make sure it was safe to leave her for a few minutes. It was. *Solveig* was bowling along before a northeaster which occasionally gusted 25 knots. The main was the only sail set, strapped down to starboard, and there was no other vessel in sight. Every now and then a big one got beneath her, slaloming her in a flurry of foam, with the log nudging 10 knots. The wind-vane was handling it perfectly, steering her true with unfailing devotion to duty. The sky was blue and, except for the blossoming whitecaps, so was the sea. After beating against a southeasterly,

Wrongful arrest

mostly in rain squalls, for the 1,000-odd miles from Cairns in Queensland to Cape Byron, it was possible to see advantages in New South Wales. Satisfied with life, I went below.

Lunch was sardine sandwiches. I had barely sunk my teeth into the first of them when things started to go wrong.

It wasn't a dramatic beginning, just an ill-defined feeling that the cutter's motion had altered. Thinking I must be imagining things, I took a look through one of the starboard windows. The New South Welsh coastline, until then sliding satisfactorily past, had come to a stop. Going up and down, it could manage, sliding past, it seemed, was too much. A wave broke over the transom, flooding the cockpit.

We looked at each other. *Solveig* is Tasmanian and it blows a bit down there. She is also notoriously dry. Water like that had never come on board, even during any of the innumerable Bass Strait gales we have sailed her through. We had rather given up thinking it ever might.

Then it happened again, cascades of water pouring into the cockpit and gurgling enthusiastically down the drains. A slurp or two even found its way over the washboards, breaking the paralysis of surprise and driving us up to the deck.

It didn't take more than a glance over the side to see what had happened. We had been caught up by a loop of polypropylene line which had jammed itself between the boat's skeg and the balance section of her rudder. On the port side, where it fastened the boat to the sea bed at an angle, it was bar-taut. On the starboard side, it ended in a cluster of buoys and a marker flag, all of which had been submerged. Presumably a gale had driven the pot, to which the line was no doubt connected, into a crevice and jammed it there.

What astonished me was how thin that line was. It had stopped seven tonnes of boat travelling at 8 knots or so and was now holding her against wind and sea with the main still filling. I wouldn't have believed it possible.

Another wave broke over the transom and water swirled around our bare knees.

'You'll have to cut it,' my wife said with her usual conviction, glancing over the side into the transparent blue depths.

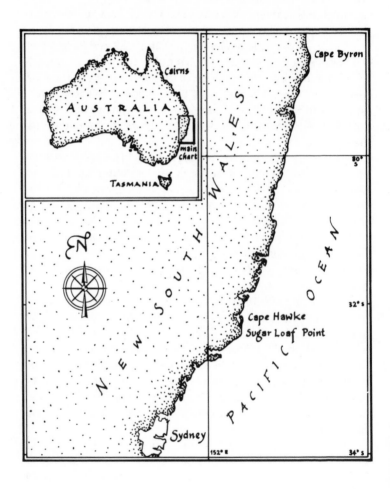

I tried the tiller. Depressingly, as I expected, it was jammed. Under those circumstances, cutting that line didn't seem too good an idea to me. To be candid, I really didn't fancy the prospect of drifting down on to Seal Rocks with a jammed rudder. Life is too good. Besides, *Solveig* is the only boat we've got, or are ever likely to have. I pointed this out to her.

'Maybe it'll work loose when the strain's off?' she suggested.

Well, maybe. And then again, maybe not. And if the latter, what then?

'We can't stay here forever,' she said.

She was right. It would get very boring. Not to mention the odd wave flooding the cockpit every few minutes and the wine supply needing renewing.

'So *you* think of something!' she said, huffily, after I expressed agreement.

Not being heroic, I didn't want to accept the obvious conclusion, but there seemed no alternative. 'I'll have to go over the side,' I told her.

She gave me one of her looks. 'Out here!' she exclaimed. 'You can't! I won't let you.'

Well, it was touching, wasn't it? After all these years, too. Touching, but not altogether realistic. 'The booze'll run out,' I pointed out.

She paled. 'Oh my God!'

'I knew you'd see it my way,' I said.

The first thing to do seemed to be to get the sail down; an effort involving considerable blasphemy, bearing in mind that it was full of 20-odd knots of breeze and we were being held firmly before the wind in a Bermudian-rigged boat. We clawed it down, persuaded it to desist from its insane desire to wrap itself around the shrouds, and finally got it lashed to the boom.

My wife looked over the side and turned back, biting her lip. 'It looks horribly dangerous,' she said, stating the obvious.

I got a harness on, lengthened it with a few metres of rope, shoved the rope ladder over the side, found the face mask and snorkel and tied a knife to my wrist.

She looked at me. 'Oh hell!' she said, close to tears, and gave me a kiss. I looked at her a long moment then spat in the mask,

swilled it with seawater from the plentiful supply in the cockpit, put it on and went down the ladder.

She was right about one thing. It was dangerous. The back end of the boat was rising and falling three or four metres and each time it came down it hit the sea with a blow like a sledgehammer, sending up sheets of spray. I didn't much fancy being under there when that happened. There was a shortage of neurosurgeons in the immediate vicinity.

I swam round behind the boat's stern and, seizing my moment, dived and cut the marker flag and buoys off the line, leaving a free end about a metre and a half long. I waited around for a quiet patch and, when it came, picked up the fall and dived right under the boat, swimming beneath keel and skeg and surfacing on the port side.

I now had both ends of the loop on the same side of the boat and, bracing my feet against the skeg, heaved as hard as I could on the free end whilst Johanna tried pushing and pulling the tiller. The trouble was that I kept having to go up for air and when I got to the surface and blew the snorkel clear I'd inhale seawater from the spray of the boat slamming down close to my head. Several times I had to hang on to the rope ladder and cough and gasp water out of my lungs.

The rope was shifting though. Little by little, we worked it out of the joint between the skeg and the balanced forward end of the rudder until, after what seemed like a hundred attempts, it finally gave.

I was very glad of the lifeline and it wasn't just because I was half-drowned and very tired. Freed from the restraint of the polypropylene line, the boat started moving, towing me behind her. She was going too fast for me to do much more than simply put up with it, but my wife glanced over the back and when she had enough steerage way put the helm down and swung the boat across the wind, enabling me to grab the rope ladder.

Even with her help, it seemed a long way up the side and when I was finally back in the cockpit I was incapable of doing much more than gasp and splutter for a good ten minutes.

She looked down at me, lying there with water pouring out of me, and shook her head. 'Boring,' she said. 'Completely boring.'

I suppose you'll think we deserved it, going cruising in a boat with a balanced rudder. Maybe you'd be right, too, but then again, they're all a compromise and I've seen equally strange misfortunes befall conventional boats.

When conditions are really bad, there isn't a boat I'd sooner be in, so I guess we'll hang on to *Solveig*. She's wooden, too. Neither of us can stand the smell of the plastic ones.

It is a risk though, especially on that New South Wales coast. There are literally thousands of those pots for miles out to sea and quite a few of them have flags and buoys submerged. Certainly not one of them is lit at night. We were lucky in a way. Suppose it had been dark when it happened?

Alan Bond has been sailing since childhood and lives in Queensland, Australia. An anaesthetist by profession, he says: 'When I got to be 50, we did what we always said we would . . . I resigned from my practice and we sold the house and went to live on the boat.' It was just before the stockmarket crash. After 18 carefree months he and his wife, Johanna, were driven back to the rat race. A year was enough to cure them of that idea and last reports indicated that, although living frugally, they planned to return to life aboard Solveig, *a 36ft wooden cutter. A circumnavigation was also talked about . . .*

Swanning across Sweden

by *Julaine Cleland*

I don't normally do the laundry at three o'clock in the morning, but this *was* the height of summer, and the golden ray of sunrise flashing across the blue sky imitated the fluttering flags of our host country, Sweden.

Sweden rates very high in everyone's book as a place to cruise. The icy, blue-green, rock-speckled water keeps the sailor excited. The naturalist is delighted with the pristine islands and forests and the abundant bird life. The galley-slave is enthralled with the always accessible fresh provisions, the beautiful bakeries, and the sparkling marinas, with their comprehensive facilities.

We were four aboard our Vancouver 36, *Tropic Bird*, which had been home for my husband Robert and me for three years. We had sailed her from America to England and spent spring and early summer cruising England's south coast. Then it was across the Channel, through the flower-decked canals of Holland, across the corner of the North Sea, and through the Kiel Canal. The fairytale islands of Denmark were followed by the boulder-strewn archipelago of southern Sweden and the Åland Islands of Finland, before making our way back into Stockholm's Wasa Marina. Here we picked up my sister and brother-in-law, Jan and Pete Carroll. They are experienced and enthusiastic sailors, as well as good fun.

We spent several days enjoying the islands of Stockholm, but now we were ready to take on the Göta Canal, the start of a passage back towards England, and rumoured to be the highpoint of everybody's trip to the Baltic.

After a wet and windy start, day after glorious day dawned beautiful and sunny as we enjoyed one of the nicest summers most Swedes could remember.

On the first day of August we entered the first lock of the Göta Canal. After fifty Dutch locks, we thought we had worked out a good system, but these tiny, hand-operated, 150-year-old locks were as different from the big mechanised ones of Holland as the slender, winding little Göta was from the bustling barge-strewn Rhine. Fortunately, the lock attendants are experienced and helpful as the lift in most of the chambers is very high, 8ft to 10ft, and the water floods in with the swirl and turbulence of a washing machine.

Jan and I set off to check out the village, while Robert and Pete watched the boats in line ahead of us negotiate the first lock, and observed each crew's method of coping with the cascade. They devised a routine that worked well for us, and we were glad to have four sets of hands and every fender aboard to help out. Each had his specific duties; with Robert steering, we would pull up to the landing at the base of the lock and Pete, with a 100ft bow line, and I, with a short stern line, would jump ashore. Jan would stay aboard amidships to keep us fended off the low stone banks. The shore crew would tow *Tropic Bird* into the lock and while the stern was tied up with as short a lead as possible, the end of the bow line was secured well forward of the boat and led down to a snatch block at the stem head and back to a genoa winch in the cockpit, where the slack was taken up as the water flooded in. When the top of the lock was reached, the shore party either hopped back aboard or pulled the boat on into the next lock of a staircase.

We sorted ourselves out into a lock-full of boats, and a very mixed bag we were. *Tropic Bird* would go through the front of the lock on the starboard wall, with *African Queen*, a beautiful cus-tom-built Swan 46, from Bremen, Germany, on the port side. Between us, we filled the forward end of the lock so completely that the two smaller Swedish and Dutch boats behind were pro-tected from the torrent. This was our little floating United Nations. We managed our first three locks successfully and tied up along-side in Söderköping, a beautiful old town full of lovely flowers, shady trees, verdant lawns, and cobbled streets. We soon got better acquainted with Ute and Uwe Geisler, from *African Queen*, and Rolf Nilsson in his yet-unnamed boat from Göteborg. These were friendships that would last much longer than the passage through the canal. Besides our own little international group, we had the company of a traditional 90ft wooden schooner from Swedish National Television. An on-board cast and many support vehicles were to travel with us, filming a live two-hour programme every evening that featured the beauty and history of the canal and the life of the people along its banks. We had not expected to star in a major television production.

The next day's journey was only 12 miles to Norsholm, but included eleven locks and seven bridges. After so much hopping on and off, *Tropic Bird* was much in need of a good scrub, and we demonstrated our skills as 'swabbies' for the cameras.

Our first open water experience was Lake Roxen, between Norsholm and Berg, and it was just long enough to justify putting up the sails before we took our places in line to ascend our first six-chamber staircase. The set of locks is a local tourist attraction, and many people came to have lunch and view the unusual sight of boats climbing 50ft up a mountain. The tourists were frequently fascinated by our American flag, and questioned us often: 'Have you really come all the way from America in that little boat?'

Finally, it was our turn to make the ascent. Our flotilla distin-guished itself with panache, so we brashly decided to take on a few more double locks. Closing time at 1800 hours found us at a little landing stage in the rural farmlands of central Sweden. Here we dined under the placid gaze of cows artistically arranged in a golden field splattered with scarlet poppies.

The countryside changed again, as the banks were lined with huge old trees; oaks, elms, linden and white birch. We took

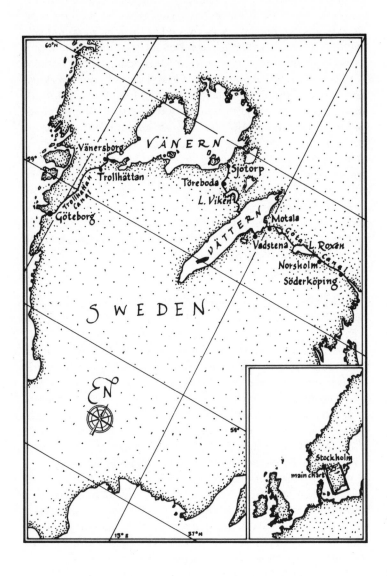

thirteen locks in our stride, including another six-chamber stair-case, and breezed across Lake Boren, arriving in Motala, the old headquarters of the Göta Canal Company. Next morning Lake Vättern lay spread before us and we had the advantage of a fair wind. Further on, Vadstena's medieval bricks and stone basked in the rosy glow of the afternoon sun as we took up our slip in the moat of the fifteenth-century castle, and prepared to breach the walls, armed with guidebooks and cameras. Dinner at the Radhus was followed by a romantic stroll through the long, lingering twilight of Nordic summer. The west wind was just chilly enough to make us glad to reach *Tropic Bird's* snug cabin.

Vadstena is too good to rush away from, so we slept late, and spent a day lazing around, each doing his own thing, but all taking in the magnificent sixteenth-century cathedral and monastery with their biblical wood carvings. Books read, letters written, naps taken, we were ready to welcome our American friends Geoff and Phoebe on *Bidarka*, whom we first met in Holland. With one exception they were the only American boat we saw all summer. In the late afternoon we revelled in a great American feast of real hotdogs and ice cream. The wind obligingly died off, leaving a warm, lustrous evening to reminisce of other sails in other waters, knowing this was also one to be savoured later.

The next day we were back to our hydraulic highway. We went through our last 'up' lock, the oldest in the system, built in 1813, and the one with the highest lift, 11.5ft. We also reached the highest elevation on the Göta, 301 feet above sea level. Not, however, a record height for *Tropic Bird,* since we built her in the mountains of West Virginia.

We made lazy progress along this beautiful section of the canal, trying to stretch out the inevitable ending of this adventure. The narrow, winding channel opened out into Lake Viken and we explored every inch of it, finally finding the ultimate anchorage in a tiny green bower of fir and birch trees, watched over by a tra-ditional Swedish red and white summerhouse. The peace and solitude were so absolute that even conversation seemed an intrusion.

We left our verdant nest with great sadness and began the downward part of our journey across Sweden. The descending

locks are so easy in comparison, particularly when you know the trick of partially filling your fenders with water so they won't float uselessly when the water level is right at the top of the wall.

An early stop at Toredoba put us at a dock directly in front of the tourist information office and next door to the train station; perfect for Jan and Pete to make their departure for Germany, returning reluctantly to the reality of jobs and children. With sad goodbyes still salty on our cheeks, we continued down a canal that seemed to grow ever smaller and more remote from the ordinary world. The green and tranquil scenery was perhaps the most beautiful we'd seen. We wondered what it would be like in the middle of winter.

Spending the night at Lyrestad gave us eight locks apiece for each of the last two days, and allowed us to plan on making the 0900 bridge opening in town. The last eight locks dropped us down to the level of Lake Vänern at Sjötorp, the official end of the Göta Canal. Vänern is one of the largest lakes in Europe, and even after that there is still the Trollhätte Canal to lower you down to sea level and sweep you into Göteborg.

We paused at Sjötorp only to hand in our papers, then motored on a hot, breathless, bronze mirror out to the island of Kållandso, to stay in the moat of yet another castle, Läcko. Somehow we had tired of castles, and never even went inside this one, preferring to spend the evening with our Swedish friend Rolf Nilsson, who regaled us with the delights in store for us in Göteborg.

Another long day of motoring brought us to the end of the open water at Vänersborg. We negotiated a couple of bridges in the Trollhätte, and then the first of the six locks of this very different canal. The lock chambers were huge, like motoring into a small rectangular lake. The drop was enormous, 25ft to 30ft, and by now the wind had piped up to a shrill, freezing-wet blast: this was not at all what we had in mind. The guest harbour, just beyond the lock, looked very welcoming, but without a doubt, autumn was starting to close in on Scandinavia, and we were heading in the right direction.

The next day, with small freighters for companions and cold, blustery rain for accompaniment, we covered five more huge locks and a canal lined with scrap-metal yards and chemical plants. This was not the kind of treatment we had grown to expect from Sweden's canals. We slunk into Göteborg, grimy, wet and bedraggled, to discover a splendid city with the guest harbour literally in the middle of town. We'd finally made it. And as if to prove it, all our friends we'd made along the Göta were lined up on the dock to greet us.

American Julaine Cleland, a retired graphic artist, and her husband, Robert, moved aboard Tropic Bird, *their Vancouver 36, in 1986 after two years work completing their cruising home. Robert decided to take retirement at 50 from a successful career as a chemical engineer. 'We couldn't stand another eight-hour drive to the boat, so it seemed the right time to go,' says Julaine. After a year spent honing their skills from 20 years of holiday and weekend sailing, they crossed the Atlantic, pausing in Bermuda, the Azores and Ireland, before exploring Europe.*

It's all in the mind

by *June Elford*

A wig and an oilskin hood are not compatible. I discovered this as I sat in the cockpit of a boat and experienced the initial pangs of seasickness. With the tide ebbing westwards we had reached the point of no return at the Fairway buoy off the Isle of Wight. How did I get into this miserable situation?

We were sailing to Cherbourg and then on to Alderney. Nothing unusual about that unless your skipper is a doctor who is determined to cure you of seasickness. He was convinced a lot of it was psychological: if you think you are going to be sick, you will be. The whole idea of the trip was to prove his theory. I was then 'press-ganged' into going by the other members of the crew. They swept aside my protests with the lack of feeling to be found in those totally absorbed with the problem of bringing home their duty-frees.

But why wear a wig? Was this part of the cure? I decided if I had to go, I would at least look glamorous. Most women who sail appreciate the damage the wind does to their hair. It ends up a straggly, salty mess. A friend, who looks immaculate when sail-

ing, suggested a wig. Wear it to protect your hair, she said, or pop
it on when you arrive. Either way you'll look good. Unfortunately
the wig turned out to be a mass of dark curls which no amount of
brushing could straighten. As we left the mooring in Cowes on
Friday evening, I crept below and put it on. No one remarked on
it, which was surprising as I now looked like a black sheep
wearing a yellow oilskin.

We sailed out of the Medina river and the shelter of the harbour. The water in the Solent was messy, a legacy of the previous
day's bad weather. Soon, the Needles lighthouse slipped away
behind us as the boat rose on the large waves and slid down into
dark green troughs. Since part of the experiment was to not use
anti-seasickness pills, I was feeling decidedly queasy. A recom-
mendation to stare at the horizon was no help. My oilskin hood
pushed the wig over my face as I rummaged desperately for a
bucket in the locker. Obnoxious smells of tarred string added to
the nausea. Nelson was supposed to have suffered from *mal de
mer*; I wondered, fleetingly, how he coped. But I'm not a fighter,
I'm a coward. I stuffed the wig in the locker amongst the assortment of tackle, grabbed the bucket and staggered below to my
bunk.

I thought the long night would never end. Once I woke from
an uneasy doze to hear the thud of footsteps on the deck above.

'There's a ship coming,' I heard them call. 'Don't think they've
seen us.'

'Shine the torch on the sail,' came the urgent answer. I prepared myself for a watery grave. At one point the block jammed
at the top of the mast and someone had to go up to release it. The
language used to describe the boat and its faults would have done
credit to any seafaring parrot's vocabulary.

It was comforting to know that they had looked at me now and
then to see if I was still alive. They were eating their breakfast
when they told me that; plates heaped with eggs and bacon. We
were moored on the marina, having reached Cherbourg at about
0700 hours. Fishing boats chugged past and a few people were
working on the quay. I sipped a cup of tea and casually let slip
that I wanted to go back on the ferry. Not a chance: like the Flying Dutchman, I was doomed to sail forever, condemned to finish

the voyage. Secretly, I made plans to fly home from Alderney. Meanwhile I went in search of ginger biscuits, the only thing I fancied in the way of food. There were *crêpes* in abundance, *galettes* and macaroons, but no ginger biscuits. I would have to wait until we got to Alderney.

There was a welcome reprieve whilst we explored Cherbourg. This was my first visit and I remember the tall houses with their shuttered windows, the flower market ablaze with colour and the cafes and bars with people outside, enjoying a glass of wine in the sun. One hot afternoon we walked up the hill behind the town to the fort, which is now a museum. It reminded us of *Beau Geste* and we could almost believe that legionnaires would guard the gateway with the bodies of dead comrades propped against the crenellations to fool the enemy.

During our stay fog hung around the harbour, not unusual for the summer months, but after two days the forecast improved and on Tuesday we left for Alderney.

The others had talked about rocks, overfalls and the Alderney Race. I thought this was rather unwise: after all, I was supposed to have this anxiety problem about being sick. There were also the terrible stories I had heard in pubs about the tidal race. Even allowing for fifty per cent exaggeration, they could still dampen any desire to go near it. We had passed Omonville la Rogue and the Cherbourg Peninsula was coming up fast. Already I could see the ripples which mark the edge of this notorious bit of water. Then, with what I suspect was a masterly piece of psychology, I was told to watch for rocks from the bows. If there is a cure for seasickness it is sheer, unadulterated fear . . . I kept my eyes on the sea, searching for the long, brown rocks which they said looked like a turtle's back. The tide was slack and the whirlpools turned out to be small eddies. In the clear water we saw the hump of Alderney, although we were still some distance away. Quenard Point lighthouse appeared and later the long breakwater running out to sea. We found the Old Harbour beacon as our leading mark with St Anne's Church and tacked in. The weather was good by Alderney standards, but there was still a bit of a swell on the mooring once we were in Braye Harbour. I was glad to get ashore and start to discover the island.

It's all in the mind

Alderney was everything I had been promised. One of my favourite memories is the smell of hay and wild flowers mingling with warm salt air blowing off the sea. Pink seathrift grew in drifts on the cliffs and the sea was a deep blue as it surged round the jagged rocks below. We cycled round the island the next day, taking a picnic lunch to Corblets Bay, where the sand had been washed golden clean. Evening sunsets silhouetted ships against the sky as they passed the island. We strolled down to Clonque Fort to look at the Swinge, with pleasant thoughts of a visit to the Divers' Inn afterwards.

One thing was missing. There were no ginger biscuits in the shops until the cargo boat arrived with fresh supplies. My plea to be allowed to fly back to England was ignored and I was hustled past the Aurigney airline office in the main street. When we left Alderney in the early hours of Friday a deep bellow from the lighthouse siren followed us into the dense fog. I was soon back with the red bucket in a horizontal position on the bunk. The thud of ships' engines seemed to come from every direction. Overhead, the damp sails slapped as they tried to catch the light breeze. We sailed through the North Channel in the late evening and the Isle of Wight had never looked so good. Before we reached Cowes, someone found the wig lurking in the depths of the locker; it resembled a weird sea creature and caused momentary panic.

After my initiation into long-distance sailing, I discovered that nine out of ten people suffer from seasickness, and women are more susceptible than men. I had started thinking about being sick long before the balance organs in my ear were at odds with the motion of the boat. But that anxiety could be controlled with anti-sickness tablets. I also realised my attitude to sailing had changed because I was beginning to sense the feeling of achievement it brings. I was actually beginning to enjoy it. The doctor's diagnosis had been right: it is all in the mind.

June Elford, 61, is a writer who no longer sails but watches the passing parade of yachts with envy from her home in Cowes, Isle of Wight. Her boats have included a 30ft Kemrock Channel, a Kestrel 22 and a Cheverton 27.

Alaskan interlude

by *Margaret Pickering*

Charlie, my husband, pointed to a lone tropic bird, the last reminder of our two months in the Hawaiian Islands. Enthusiasm and excitement gripped us both as we headed from Honolulu for south-east Alaska in our 32ft sloop *Keegenoo* ; the name is Eskimo for 'my home'.

We had first heard of Glacier Bay in Alaska six years before, when we were in the Canary Islands. An American couple, whose boat also had an Eskimo name, graphically described that remote part of the world and inspired us to go and visit a land that, only 200 years ago, was covered in a layer of ice 4,000ft thick.

The 28-day passage from Honolulu to Sitka, from tropical heat to the icy cold of the north, was a voyage of contrasts. In and out of a 700-mile band of fog, sometimes in a stiff breeze; then, during a sudden gale, wallowing in four hours of calms only to plunge again into the raging gale. Rough and tough sailing it was, into the windswept waters of the infamous gulf of Alaska, known as the 'cradle of storms'.

The hospitality of the Pacific north-west is legendary and, 300 miles out from Sitka, a distant vessel changed course and the crew waved and sounded the ship's horn as it sped towards us. *Marlin*, the supply vessel from Seattle to Kodiak Island, stopped engines and we hove to in the heavy swell. Her skipper excitedly told us that we were the first sailing boat he had ever seen in the Gulf of Alaska. Although we needed no supplies, he insisted on lowering a sack of fresh fruit and milk, secured to a large black float, before the *Marlin* resumed its original course.

Our expected landfall, on 6 July, was the snow-capped peak of Mount Edgecumbe (3,270ft). Visibility was very poor, but the mist lifted momentarily to reveal the characteristic conical shape welcoming us; just as it must have welcomed Captain Cook on the *Resolution* in 1778. At 0600 we were at the entrance to Sitka Sound. From there, we wound our way through the archipelago of wooded islands into friendly Thomsen Harbour in Sitka, arriving at nightfall.

Historic Sitka, in the Alaskan Panhandle, was the old Russian capital from 1804 to 1867 and there the deal was struck in which Russia sold the vast territory of Alaska to the United States for two cents an acre. The Russian era is recalled by the imposing onion-shaped dome of St Michael's Orthodox Church, which dominates the town and boasts a unique collection of gold and silver icons and holy paintings, dating from Czarist times. By contrast, the strong and ancient Indian influence is seen in the impressive array of totem poles at the Sitka National Park.

The Indian summer we enjoyed during our 19-day stay in Sitka ended in drizzle and *Keegenoo*, loaded with gifts, including Dungeness crab, venison and fresh salmon, motored out of the harbour into the mist of Sitka Sound. As we went, we knew we would never forget the kindness and generosity of the people we had come to know.

Many ships have been lost near Sitka. Kalinin Bay, a secure all-weather anchorage, is named after the acting master of the Russian ship *Neva*, which foundered on rocks off Sitka Point below Cape Edgecumbe, and this, after passing through the narrow Olga Strait into Neva Strait, was to be our first call on the way to Glacier Bay.

When we anchored, the weather forecast was predicting 25 knots from the south-west, and by nightfall there were

22 fishing boats in the bay; yet more were to come by morning, seeking shelter from the worsening conditions. Around us were seals, otters and scores of different sea birds; we could hear the melancholy cry of the loon, whose ability to dive to great depths for fish never ceased to astound.

Bad weather forced us to stay an extra day and we rowed the dinghy out to the salmon collection centre, a wide barge, where the fishermen off-loaded and weighed their catch. We were invited aboard to see the mountains of salmon stored in flaked ice and there we met our first full-blooded Eskimo. That evening he brought his small fishing boat alongside *Keegenoo* to have supper and tell us enthralling tales of the harsh way of life in the frozen wastes of the north.

Glacier Bay was beckoning. Early next morning we weighed anchor, and by 1000 the sun had managed to penetrate the early mist. It was low tide and ugly rocks were visible in the exceedingly narrow channel leading from the bay. We were glad of the careful attention to detail which had been so necessary to take us safely in only two days before. We sailed alongside Chichagof Island, where on 17 July 1741 the first European ship to arrive sent 15 men ashore; they never returned, presumably butchered by the local Indians.

The west coast of Chichagof abounds in spectacular scenery, which we enjoyed before making our way through Ogden Passage, along the east side of Herbert Graves Island, to our second anchorage at Shimshan Cove. Scattered crab traps were a hazard and we cautiously edged our way into this marvellous cove, its sheltered waters a placid lake. The derelict buildings of the once lucrative Golden Gate Goldmine were on the south shore of the cove, reminding us of past prospecting days. All now was peace and tranquillity.

The Alaskan Panhandle has the greatest world concentration of bald eagles, the national emblem of the United States, and these magnificent birds gave us great pleasure as we watched them wheel high above us, ever ready to swoop on any fish careless enough to swim too close to the surface. Regretfully, at dawn, we tore ourselves away and motored into the narrow channels, assisting our small 10hp engine by raising the mainsail to catch any

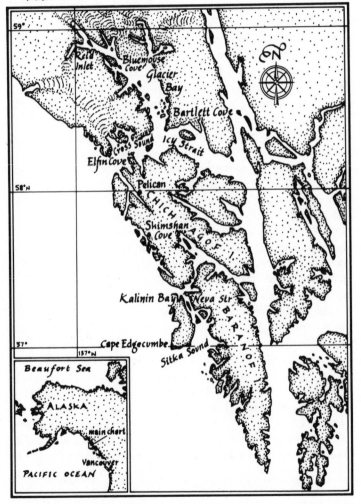

Alaskan Interlude - Pickering

59°
Reid Inlet
Bluemouse Cove
Glacier Bay
Bartlett Cove
Cross Sound
Icy Strait
Elfin Cove
58°N
Pelican
CHICHAGOF
Shimshan Cove
Kalinin Bay
Neva Str
BARANOF
Cape Edgecumbe
Sitka Sound
57°
137°W

Beaufort Sea
ALASKA
main chart
Vancouver
PACIFIC OCEAN

breeze blowing down the gullies. As we motored in a flat sea through Surveyor Passage, I was idly watching a floating log when it suddenly moved; we had disturbed a huge basking sea-lion.

Our journey north took us almost to the end of Chichagof Island and then into Lisiansky Strait. This fjord-like strait, six miles long, was explored by Captain Lisiansky, of the ill-fated *Neva*, who was the first to see the spruce-covered mountains towering above us on either side. As we came to the half-way point, we were thrilled to see a sea-otter lying on his back, his forepaws on his chest; later we saw many more around the rich kelp beds. We turned south into Lisiansky Inlet for five miles, towards the city of Pelican, which hums with activity in the fishing season. Pelican, population 167, is a boardwalk town with a city hall, a general store, tiny post office, laundromat and an old whorehouse which was up for sale. Rosie's Bar is the city nightspot, but when we were there it was quiet; only one fight, one knock-down and one fisherman parading almost naked along the bar counter. Rosie herself was buxom and smiling, a formidable opponent when challenged to play pool. The loser had to ring the huge brass bell and pay for drinks all round. Only a few patches on the ceiling lacked signatures, the bar counter and the walls were already full, and Charlie stood on the counter to write our names there.

The inland waterways of south-east Alaska, a maze of islands, inlets, caves and fiords, with over 6,000 miles of coastline, could take years to explore. On 30 July, mindful that the area is littered with wrecks, we motored towards the mouth of Lisiansky Inlet and on to our next stop. More sea-otters were playing in the kelp at the south end of Three Hills Island and the colourful puffins entertained us by diving at our approach. Suddenly, the tiny entrance to Elfin Cove revealed itself; we rounded a red marker and followed the line of buoys into the harbour. Elfin Cove, another quaint settlement of walkways, tucked along the inner reaches of a steep-sided cove, has a permanent population of 30 all the year round, plus the fishermen in the summertime. Snow-covered mountains surround the tiny cove and Brady Glacier is visible on a clear day.

Bartlett Cove was our next destination, where permission to go further into Glacier Bay has to be sought from the National Park

Service. It was cold and overcast as we motored, with mainsail up, through the South Indian Pass, passing Idaho Inlet, named after the steamship *Idaho*, which turned into the inlet in 1884, mistaking it for Lisiansky Strait, and ran aground. Such incidents from the past were a constant reminder that the region, some of it uncharted, is dangerous, a graveyard for ships. Lemesurier Island lay to starboard, and seals eyed us with curiosity; by 1300 we were inside Glacier Bay, only three miles from Bartlett Cove. Glacier Bay is frequented by killer whales and it is also a feeding ground for the hump-backed whale, two of which welcomed us to Bartlett Cove.

The 4,400 square miles of the Glacier Bay National Monument includes a host of snow-clad peaks and no less than 16 large glaciers, as well as a myriad of delightful coves, inlets and islands, offering an amazing variety of wildlife. Strict rules of entry are understandably imposed by the National Parks Service. The number of powered vessels allowed in the bay at any one time is severely limited to minimise any disturbance to the hump-back, an endangered species. All visitors are asked not to approach closer than half a mile to the whales. We were amused since in our experience, whales, hump-backed or not, seemed not to know the half mile rule!

The Park Service issued our permit and solemnly gave us their leaflets, including a warning leaflet about bears. Both black and brown bears are common in this part of the world. The leaflets said they could not be outrun and that confrontation should be avoided by singing loudly, ringing a bell or by rattling stones in a can. The leaflet advised: '. . . if the bear charges you, freeze, facing the bear. Most charges are bluffs. The bear will probably stop and run away. If it does not stop, drop to the ground and play dead . . .'

The leaflet went on to say that any self-respecting bear would then lose interest and go away.

We had strained our eyes on our journey north trying to spot a bear ashore, but a crowd of us saw a black bear from the jetty at Bartlett Cove. He was ambling along a narrow track following a line of nature ramblers led by a Ranger. Luckily none of them noticed him and the bear finally wandered off into the bush.

Alaskan interlude

Thirty miles into Glacier Bay lay Blue Mouse Cove, very well protected although the wind can blow strongly from the peaks and into the inlets. We left Bartlett Cove on full flood, in misty conditions, taking bearings the whole time. Willoughby Island, and then Drake Island, were to starboard. The latter is the site of a Hoonah Indian fort, providing evidence of early Indian activity in the bay.

Low-lying fog was an ever present threat and taking constant bearings, we were relieved to round the two islands guarding the entrance to Blue Mouse Cove. We anchored in 26-28ft and, when the fog lifted, we were looking at a remarkable Christmas card mountain scene. Fortunately, the next morning was without fog, though it was still overcast. Wild strawberries were growing in profusion on the beach and we went in our dinghy to gather them. About a mile along the beach we found a pile of steaming bear droppings, and smelt the tang of freshly crushed greenery. Instantly we forgot the strawberries. Trying not to panic and run, singing loudly to keep the bear at bay, our pace quickened as we narrowed the gap between us and the dinghy.

The following day was miserable with monotonous drizzle as we left Blue Mouse Cove early, hoping to reach Reid Inlet before dusk. A cruise liner, lights ablaze in the hazy visibility, overtook us and disappeared into the misty rain.

By 0900 ice was forming in small lumps all around us and I was leaning over the pulpit to direct our passage through. We hugged the coastline in persistent fog and, in a strong, adverse current, progress was slow. Seals bobbed around us, cheerful in a cheerless sea.

Icebergs loomed and by 1000 we had sighted three, two small and darkish, and one large and glistening white. We steered well clear, knowing that they could overturn without warning. Charlie was forced to steer completely off course now, as ice was floating in larger chunks all around us. One massive piece to starboard was as large as a medium-sized cabin cruiser.

An hour later the lumps had become huge and jagged blocks of floating ice. It was just three miles to the anchorage in Reid Inlet when we sighted the biggest iceberg yet – a grotesque monster from another world. Charlie was bending and stretching, clapping

A cruising anthology

his hands to keep warm, but I was cosy in the hatchway, relishing the welcome heat from the engine.

Shoals extended from either side of the entrance to Reid Inlet, so we were careful to open up the entrance and enter in mid-channel. The glacier suddenly appeared. It was breathtaking.

It seemed so close I felt I could touch it, and instinctively I cried out that it was unsafe to go in. From my vantage point, there seemed to be nothing there but masses of ice and towering cliffs of snow.

We nosed slowly into the inlet. Ugly rocks were visible close to us to starboard. All of a sudden the engine faltered. Charlie quickly discovered we had sprung a diesel leak and he stood over the engine, keeping it going, while I took the tiller to take *Keegenoo* in. I steered this way and that to avoid the floating broken ice, until at last we were through and able to select a spot to drop the anchor. As we went we disturbed countless guillemots, scoters and glaucous-winged gulls and we heard oyster catchers calling. Seals stared, their eyes big and brown. The skies cleared miraculously, revealing magic pinnacles of ice, the glacier gleaming in turquoise splendour. Icebergs floated below it and some were stranded, like huge whales, on the beach.

Mist soon clamped down on the glacier's summit, swirling into the inlet. The water was polished and glassy, the icebergs motionless. We hoped the fog would clear, but if not, those few exquisite moments of glorious sunlit beauty were themselves worth the journey. Harry Reid's 1890 map of the inlet, bearing his name, shows nothing but ice here. No land at all. Even in the 1940s, when Joe and Muz Ibach came here to mine for gold, and built their cabin at the entrance to the glacier, it had receded no further than the curve of their beach. Now you can pass almost two miles into the inlet. Today, the glacier is advancing again, but others, elsewhere, are withdrawing. Crevasses are splitting the ice of Reid Glacier where it is pushing across the land. Almost 200ft deep, the openings are clearly visible against the sky.

Our first job was to replace the broken diesel pipe, and then we were free to wander at will on the shore, where we disturbed a brood of ptarmigan. We came upon the now derelict cabin of Joe and Muz Ibach; shrubs and plants still flourished in the rockery she once so lovingly tended. The three spruce trees Muz had planted now stood proud and tall, a fitting monument to her fortitude.

I gingerly eased myself through the half-open door and found the cabin decaying but untouched by man. Their billy cans were still there. A rough hewn table and sturdy bunks were crowded into the small space. An ancient chest lay on the uneven wooden floor and the walls were papered with pages torn from old wallpaper books. It must have been a test of endurance for this hardy couple to have fended for themselves for so many years in the wilderness.

We walked towards the glacier, a leisurely stroll past innumerable icebergs of varying shapes and sizes, some comical and others frightening, stranded on the beach by the tide. The deep aquamarine colour of the lower sections of the bergs betrayed how massive the submerged part was in comparison with the visible portion. The incoming tide was soon to refloat these monsters. The weather was kind to us and the glittering face of the mighty glacier became more magnificent as we went nearer.

The packed ice was rock hard as we climbed part way up the side of it, balancing precariously between the huge crevasses, and leaving no footsteps to betray our presence. We were alone in a wild, rugged and unspoiled land. We slept uneasily that night, a distant and thunderous rumbling echoing in our ears.

When it was time to leave, we reluctantly weighed anchor and headed towards the glacier for a last lingering glimpse of one of the greatest natural wonders of the world, before setting out to thread our way in and out, through the accumulated ice floes, to leave Reid Inlet for the return to Bartlett Cove.

Part of the glory of Glacier Bay had been revealed to us. We had anchored at the foot of a glacier, had walked on it and touched it. In Alaska, a harsh great land, unique, wild and magnificent, where spectacular scenes are commonplace, Glacier Bay and its surroundings are perhaps the most awe-inspiring of all. The Hoonah Indians, the ancestral people of Glacier Bay, simply say 'God dwells here.'

Margaret Pickering was diagnosed in the early 1970s as having Multiple Sclerosis. 'It was this,' she says 'that led to our decision to sell up and sail.' She and her husband, Charlie, knew little about sailing, but found a good instructor. Before their nine year, world-girdling cruise they were purely armchair sailors. 'We were lucky to find a boat we felt would take care of us.' Their visit to Alaska in Keegenoo, *a 32ft Alan Buchanan-designed sloop, of foam sandwich construction, followed stopovers in Gibraltar, the Canaries, Cape Town, Freemantle, Adelaide, New Zealand, Niue, Tonga, Samoa, Tahiti and Hawaii, and was followed by Canada, San Francisco, Mexico, Panama, Florida, and Chesapeake Bay. They arrived home in time for the birth of their third grandchild. Describing herself as 'a housewife', Margaret and Charlie, both 58, have now settled down to normal life in Warwickshire. Margaret's illness is still in remission and she feels it will remain so. As husband Charlie commented after a severe gale in Bass Strait, "We have been in places where the MS dare not follow."'*

Man in the sea

by *Frank Mulville*

'I don't believe in luck,' I said, 'you get from the sea what you deserve. There's a kind of bank that looks after cruising people's accounts. When you do it right you get a credit, when you do it wrong you go into the red.'

We were talking in a bar in Bequia, on a cool veranda, with a hundred yachts at anchor in the turquoise bay, the gently waving palms throwing patterns of moving shade across a white beach. 'If I wasn't lucky,' my friend said simply, 'I wouldn't be here. I fell overboard.' He was a tall, weathered man in his fifties, with a grave face, a slow smile, and a steady eye. He asked me not to mention his name if I wrote about his struggle with the ocean.

He was alone on watch early in the morning. The sun had just risen into a cloudless sky. The yacht was sailing fast, steered by her vane gear, with twin staysails spread to the Trade wind, rolling through the ocean with a long, easy gait. He went forward to the mast on his morning check of the deck, gazing up at the white sails arching high above him, at the taut symmetry of rope, wire and canvas, on the lookout for chafe, or any wear or tear. The early light was iridescent and the sails were tinged a soft pink; flying fish skimmed the wave tops, dolphins leaped and dived, threading their lithe shapes round and under the yacht's forefoot.

The yacht gave a sudden lurch, a twist to the rhythm of her motion. For a moment he lost his balance, as he stepped back against the lifeline she gave a quick roll the other way. He flung out his arms, groped wildly for any solid thing. Then he was over, tumbling backwards head first into the turbulence of the yacht's bow wave. He remembers the feeling of alarm welling up within him.

He broke surface in panic, saw the opaque, shining sides sliding past, reached upwards and grasped the yacht's rail. The water tore at his body, his shoes and his clothing, dragging him backwards and downwards. She rolled away from him. There was a drumming in his ears. He tried to shout but no sound came. He held on until his arms stretched and his fingers cracked. She rolled again, immersing him again. Slowly, deliberately, his hands were wrenched free of the rails.

He broke surface again to see the stern, the yacht's name in gold letters and the taffrail swing past. The log line was his last chance. He swam a few strokes, found it close to the surface, clutched at it with both hands.

Again the sea dragged and tore at him. The thin line slipped through his hands, pulled against his grasp with overwhelming force, burning and cutting deep weals.

For a moment he held fast to the rotator, the line twisted round his forearm. He raised his head to shout; the sea smashed into his face, his eyes, his mouth. The log line stretched bar tight, vibrating like a guitar string. He could see the fitting on the taffrail bend towards him. The line broke with a dull, resonant twang.

Suddenly he was still and the world was quiet. The yacht's trim form grew smaller and receded. He filled his lungs and shouted, but the sound of his voice was lost in the ocean, a tiny cry sent into an empty wilderness, scattered by the wind.

The fight was over, there was peace. Soon the yacht was far away, poised on the summit of the long Atlantic swells. He could see her diminished shape in relief against the sky, now in the trough, her sails bisected by the ocean, now gone. He tasted the

Man in the sea

salt in his mouth, felt the cling of the sea round his body, caught the early sun on his upturned face. The sea was warm, almost caressing now. He kicked off his shoes, allowed the broken line and the rotator to slip through his fingers, watched it snake away, carried downwards through the darkening shadow of the ocean.

He settled himself to drown. He told me he remembers being overcome by a profound peace. Hope was gone, replaced by calm acceptance. It was a good way to go, he thought as he lay on his back, gazing at the pale heaven above, without regret, without rancour, without remorse. He had lived well, he would die well.

He imagined his body a prey to the life of the ocean. Sea creatures would thrive on him as he had thrived on them. There was a ready justice in it. With a kind of detachment, he thought of people he knew and loved. They would accept his death as he accepted it, sadly perhaps, but without bitterness. His friends would forget in weeks, months, years.

He was at peace. It was as much as a man can do with his life to leave it in peace, all problems shelved at a stroke. He was prepared, even happy, to accept the inexplicable experience of his own death.

Aboard the yacht, one of the crew woke up and came out of the cabin to find the deck deserted, the log line broken. For a moment, not believing what he saw, he looked about the deck, forward, aft, below, the comprehension of disaster slowly gaining on his consciousness. Then he shouted, 'Man Overboard!' Then, more urgently, 'Quick – for Christ's sake, man overboard – he's gone!'

They tumbled from their bunks, half asleep, befuddled, the truth slowly taking hold of their minds. It took half-an-hour to turn the yacht on the wind, to dismantle the Trade Wind gear. Twins down, guys off, mains'l set, stays'l hoisted, runners taken up, sheets pinned in, helm put down. Suddenly, the easy Trade Wind motion was replaced by the crash and tumble of water on the deck and the creak and strain of a sailing vessel hard on the wind.

One man climbed aloft with binoculars and perched on the lower spreader, one plotted the track, taking the yacht in a zig-zag, no more than five minutes on each tack, to cover the ground over a reciprocal course. One steered, keeping the compass course with all his concentration. They knew it was a slender chance that they would see a figure in this vast ocean. They searched the bleak seascape and cursed their shipmate for not wearing a safety harness or a life jacket. They were gripped by fear, the terrible apprehension of sudden bereavement.

My friend has only a hazy recollection of what passed through his mind as he trod water in the warm sea. He told me it felt like being in a garden on a summer's day, the mind at rest, the soul slumbering, at ease.

After an hour he looked up from his calm contemplation and far away saw the white tip of the yacht's sail. It appeared like a fantasy, a quirk of imagination dancing among the ocean swells, up and down, in and out, behind, round and about the uneven waves. He turned in the water and looked away, his mind suddenly in disorder. Surely all was settled. What was this new confusion? He turned again, and again he saw the white sail, far away, like a white dream. At once his peace and serenity, the fearless acceptance of his fate, the deep quietude of his mind, was broken in pieces.

Now he wanted only to live. If his fight for his life was to start again he was going to win it. He struggled to keep himself afloat for just another few minutes, cursed that he had not the strength to shout louder, to lift his body higher out of the sea.

He remembered blaspheming against his friends on the yacht. The ignorant bastards were on the wrong tack. They were going further from him, the sail was getting smaller. Hopeless, useless, blind idiots – had they not the wit to come about? 'Damn their eyesight,' he shouted, 'damn them, damn them to hell.' Half in delirium he saw the yacht come round on the other tack and sail towards him again. 'Come on!' he cried, 'come on, for Christ's sake come on!'

Now he thought only of the joys of living and eating and sleeping and of all the warmth of life. He wanted to have it with every part of his being. The yacht came closer. Now he could see the hull as she lifted gracefully on the long swell, could see the spray flying over her bow, could see the man aloft.

His ordeal was over. He let out a last croaking shout that would bring them to him, raised his hand for a final wave that would guide them alongside. He could see the yacht clearly now, her white hull lifting on the seas, throwing the waves from her bow, heeling to the wind, taut and confident. He imagined strong arms reaching down for him, grasping his body in a firm, friendly grip, heaving and struggling until he was on board. He wanted to feel their arms round him, to look up into their anxious faces. Soon he would be below in the warm luxury of the cabin, drinking with his friends, thanking them with his eyes. Then the yacht came round and stood away on the other tack.

What were they doing? What were they thinking of? Were they playing with him, mocking him, joking his life away? He shouted again, more weakly now. Cruel, cynical, perverted bastards - would they drive him insane? Was there no end to this treachery?

Once again he despaired of life, but this time with bitterness and hatred in his soul. He was dying with a black heart, his own friends drowning him for their pleasure. He turned away from the white sails full of anger. He lay on his back, the sea splashing over his face, his breath weak. The fight was gone from him and the peace had gone. Only the acid flavour of defeat was left.

His friends told him that there was a look of pain on his twisted countenance when they found him, hauled him on board, expelled the water from his lungs and forced back the air of life. They gave him brandy and he slept and woke to tell me his tale. 'On your reckoning,' he said to me, 'I think I'm a bit overdrawn at the bank.'

Frank Mulville has made six solo crossings of the Atlantic in his gaff cutter Iskra, *and sailed her to Norway and round Iceland. He spent a childhood in boats in Essex and Argentina. During the war he was torpedoed in the Atlantic. Afterwards he became, in turn, a window cleaner, journalist, salesman, cookery demonstrator and businessman. A regular contributor to* Yachting Monthly, *he is the author of several books, including* Terschelling Sands, In Granma's Wake, Schooner Integrity *and* Single-handed Sailing. *He lives in Maldon. His seventh book,* Dear Dolphin, *was published this year.*

Tropical night passage

by *Maureen Girdlestone*

A tropical depression was moving across the Eastern Caribbean. We wanted to sail across to the island of St Maarten, but with such weather conditions discretion became the better part of valour. We decided to wait it out in Charlotte Amalie harbour, St Thomas, as patiently as only impatient yachtsmen can be for the weather to clear. So, while the rain came down in buckets, the swells rocked us silly and the wind howled and shrieked, we sat it out in the cabin of our 34ft Peterson sloop, *Mon Cheri*.

One morning, popping our heads out of the hatch, we found a watery blue sky, the sun battling weakly to appear. Our dampened spirits lifted. St Maarten was about 110 miles away. We would have to leave that evening, and sail through the night, to make the approach in daylight. Averaging 5 knots, it should take about 20 hours.

We sailed at sunset, in company with the giant cruise ship *Norway*. They turned west, the passengers looking forward to a night of dining, dancing, light and warmth. We turned east. For my husband, Nelson, and me, sailing double-handed, we faced a night alone in the darkness of an empty sea.

Night fell sooner than it might, since it was still overcast. We quickly warmed and ate a pre-cooked dinner and then switched on navigation lights, checking that the sails were settled. The storm had left behind a lumpy sea, and we were at times surfing along at 6-7 knots, hoping there would be no more rain showers.

Suddenly there was a loud thump. Yachtsmen don't like a noise like that. We stared at each other's shadows in the black night. With a feeling of eeriness, we realised that the boat had come to a stop. The sails were still filled with wind, but our creamy white wake, illuminated by the stern light, had vanished. What had happened?

'We must have snagged a fish pot,' said Nelson. We dodged them constantly by day, but at night they were invisible. Nelson fetched a sharp knife and leaned down over the transom to investigate.

I grasped the tiller in one had and with the other took a firm grasp on the waistband of his denims, much as I had put a re-taining grasp on my sons' pants when they were tiny. Suddenly the fish pot, helped by the swells, bounced free and, with a violent lurch, we took off with the acceleration of a powerboat.

The rest of the night began to pass uneventfully, with nothing to relieve the boredom of each long hour. The hands of my watch seemed to slow to a snail's pace. The change of each hour was greeted as one would greet a new day.

Our eyes had adjusted to night vision, but it helped little, for with no moon there was nothing to illuminate our lonely world in the overcast conditions, not even one bright, comforting star to keep us company. I decided I didn't like it one little bit. I had heard of Stygian darkness, but I had never experienced it so completely. It was like being suddenly blinded, or having a dark blanket thrown over you. The sea and sky were like black tar, not even the horizon was discernible, nor anywhere was a paler shade of grey.

The cabin lights were out and our only comfort came from the faint red glow of the compass light and the white stern light reflecting on the tumbling wake.

This was not our first night sail together. We had developed a

Girdlestone

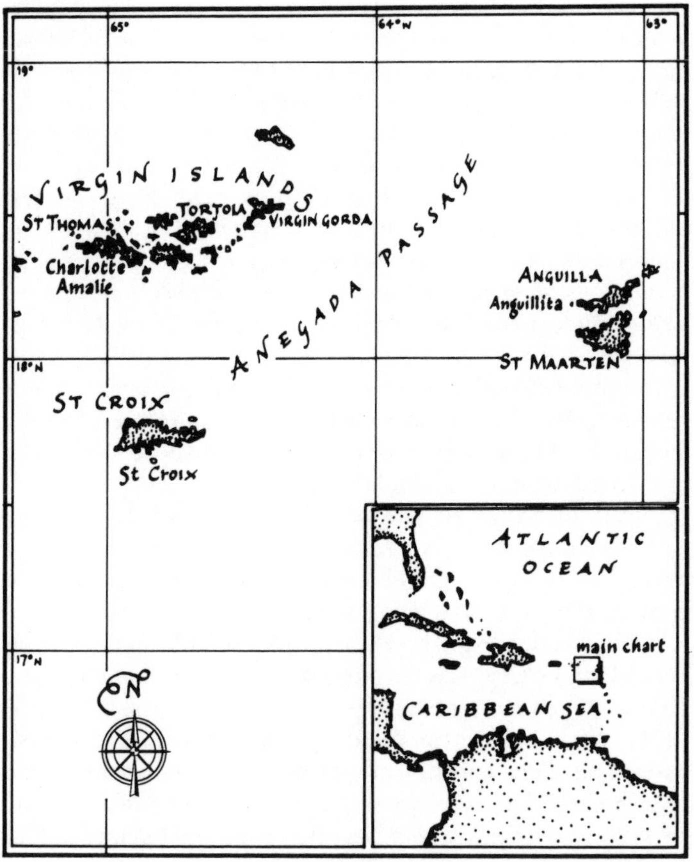

routine where we both stayed on deck all night, one napping while the other was on the helm, ever ready, in a moment of doubt, to raise a head and confirm a light, or the direction of another vessel.

We both had confidence in each other's ability to keep a steady compass course. There were many tales of people sailing in circles in the disorientation of darkness. At about 0200, when the human body is said to be at its lowest ebb, I spotted lights. I roused Nelson to confirm my assessment that it was a fishing boat, for distances are deceptive in the dark. We passed one another and it soon disappeared over the horizon, leaving us alone again.

Pangs of hunger began to attack as the night dragged slowly on. Nelson took the helm, while I went below, using my small pocket flashlight to avoid switching on cabin lights and upsetting his night vision. For snacks there were some apples, but they were a little sour for a cold dark night, or some carrots. I took the carrots up on deck and we both began munching.

Nelson stiffened. I could see his chin raised, like an animal picking up the scent on the wind. He was looking around him and then ducking in an attempt to pick up a horizon beneath the sails.

'What's wrong?' I sensed his alarm.

'I can smell land,' he said, sounding very worried.

I was on my feet, too, eyes searching for anything; a shadow in the dark which might be deeper than the rest. I could see nothing. If there was anything, it was invisible.

Nelson had sailed all his life and had several Atlantic crossings beneath his belt. He was the most experienced sailor I knew and I had faith in his judgement.

'I know the smell of land and I can smell it now . . . I am never wrong,' he added conclusively, his head constantly ducking and weaving, searching for shadows. My skin prickled with fear. Were we hurtling through the darkness to a deadly appointment with a coral reef or an outcrop of rocks?

We checked, and re-checked our course and progress. There was no way we should be near land yet. Believing in your compass is sound advice, but uncertainty and doubt overcame us. I felt the cold arms of fear embracing me. If only we could *see*. Our eyes ached to detect shape or form from the darkness.

'It could be', said Nelson, 'that we have been going far faster than we thought. Maybe the current is playing games.'

Perhaps, instead of an approach to the north-west corner of St Maarten, we had been pushed off-course and were approaching the British island of Anguilla, north of St Maarten. Or maybe it was the uninhabited, unlit islet of Anguillita. Maybe. Maybe. Maybe.

I was shivering, as much from tension as cold, and we pulled on extra jerseys and wished desperately for dawn and relief from this terrifying, black world.

We continued to keep our eyes peeled, but could still barely see our hands in front of our faces.

'Please hurry dawn,' I muttered, sinking tensely back on the cockpit seat and picking up my abandoned carrot to munch. As I bit it, sudden realisation dawned on me. I stared at the carrot in my hand. I could *smell* it. It smelled of meadows, or earth! Yes, land!

I began to laugh convulsively. It suddenly all seemed so funny, and tears rolled down my cheeks.

Nelson stared at me, bemused. 'What is it?' he demanded. Had I gone off my rocker from the strain and tension of the night? Gales of laughter swept across the deck of the little boat with its two occupants on the deserted sea.

Pointing weakly to the half-eaten carrot, I said: 'Land! T*hat's* the land you can smell!' He looked at me, at first disbelieving and then, perhaps, a trace of sheepishness.

Soon there was a paler shade of grey in the east and the blackness dissolved into the butterfly hues of a Technicolor sunrise. The sun rose majestically from the horizon to take a bow.

By mid-morning we spotted blue hills on the horizon. St Maarten was exactly where she was supposed to be. We were spot on course.

Maureen Girdlestone lives in South Africa and considers the wild seas of the Cape her home waters. She sails with her husband. When their uninsured 43ft sloop, Alter Ego, *was stolen from Cape Town, they initiated a world search and found her in Grenada, in the West Indies. 'Faced with the problem of what to do next, we threw up our jobs, recovered the boat and took up live-aboard cruising . . . it*

*proved to be the most wonderful and thrilling experience of my life,'
she says. The couple spent some time in the Caribbean doing yacht
deliveries for American owners, before moving on to the
Mediterranean for a spell.*

The loss of Gwendoline

by *Geoffrey Toye*

It was teatime on a fine Sunday afternoon in August when we sailed over the bar at Cardigan in a light north-easterly breeze. We planned to make a crossing to Dunmore East, in Southern Ireland, and conditions, it seemed, could not have been better. The forecast was good.

Gwendoline was a 19ft 6ins carvel sloop, a Sterte, designed by Fred Parker and built by Kitsons at Poole. When she came into my possession she was badly in need of a refit. Most of her ribs were cracked, her keelbolts had rusted thin as needles, and patches of her transom were soft enough to poke a finger through. It was a labour of love, and when she was relaunched every defective part had been restored.

She was a very pretty boat, white with a gold sheerline. Her boot top and deck were red, her brightwork newly varnished. She was a gleaming example of brass and mahogany, heroine of a marine survey and the darling of my eye.

Nor was she just an ornament. I remember reading about a Sterte that had crossed the Atlantic twice, and I can well believe it. During the three seasons that I sailed her, on several occasions in the sudden and violent conditions frequently found of the West Coast, I never once doubted her ability to take care of herself in bad weather. She was sometimes stubborn in stays, but she was fast, weatherly and could be trusted to steer herself on most windward courses.

For several months we had planned an Irish crossing. The plans began over a dinner at Bristol, where Tracy, my volunteer crew, was an art student. My feeling of good fortune at acquiring such an attractive crew was tempered with some doubt as to the wisdom of accepting one so inexperienced. However, she proved a remarkably quick learner and, in the event, I believe I may owe her my life. She was pleasant company, a natural sailor, and infinitely forgiving when things went wrong. If this paragon had a fault it was that she was a vegetarian. The meal she cooked us before we set sail upon the foamy wastes was a kind of undercooked dough whose Marmite aroma was reminiscent of sweet and sour All-Bran. It was awful.

Off Cemaes Head, the sea was confused. It often is, just there. I streamed the log, took the departure and arranged the chart on the plotting board, making a few calculations for the effects of tide in advance. Tracy was quiet and when I looked up from my work I noticed she appeared rather green. Coincidentally, I did not feel too wonderful myself and since I had never before been seasick, I put our mutual queasiness down to the lunch, aggravated by the choppy sea off the headland. I was soon to discover the foolishness of that piece of reasoning.

It was still light and I turned in to snatch a couple of hours before the night watch. When I awoke, night was falling and the land was well astern, the Strumble Head light clearly visible on the quarter. We chatted and shared a hot drink in the cockpit. After my nap I was feeling a little brighter, but Tracy was still sick. She took my place in the bunk.

Then followed the best sail of my life. The breeze strengthened to perhaps Force 4 and under full sail *Gwendoline* danced along, throwing up clouds of phosphorescent spray that set the sails aglow. I was wearing a reefer jacket which shone brightly as the droplets were trapped in the wool. I was startled to see the back

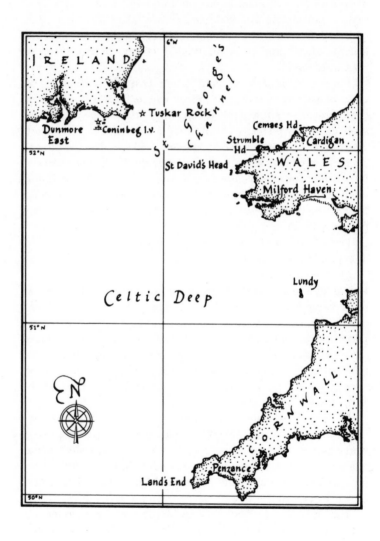

of my hand glowing, emitting enough light to illuminate surrounding objects. A steamer overhauled us and passed by a couple of cables to starboard, her lights shining brightly and her wake a blaze of phosphorescence. All of this beneath a perfect canopy of stars on a night I shall never forget.

Just before dawn, the wind began to increase. Tracy had been feeling sick most of the night, so I had left her in her bunk. However, the time had come to reef, so she took the helm while I put a couple of rolls in the main. Now Tracy was feeling better but, once again, I began to feel sick and unable to do very much.

The wind was still rising and visibility was poor. Dead reckoning put us near Tuskar Rock, although I had been unsuccessful in picking it up on the RDF. Not wishing to close that inhospitable coast in uncertain conditions, I decided to trust the DR and swing south, hoping to resume a westerly course towards the Coningbeg LV once our reckoning put us south of the rocks.

I turned in below and, just as I was dropping off to sleep, there was a severe jolt and a crunching noise from below. My first thought was that we had run on to the rocks, but Tracy could see none and the echo sounder put us in very deep water. Then there was another impact and a loud bang. The centreboard case, to which my bunk was fastened, quivered violently.

I should have sprung from my bunk and gone on deck, and sitting in my study now, years later, it seems incredible that I did not. I remained in my bunk for two reasons, or rather one reason and one cause. Tracy had announced that she could see a large fin just off the bow. By the description it must have been a mature basking shark and I guessed we must have grounded upon its back and it had responded angrily. The sighting of the fin explained the impact against the keel. It seemed futile to go on deck since there was nothing that could be done. Also, I was very sick and the lethargy which accompanies that sensation has to be experienced to be believed.

Peace returned and I fell asleep. When I awakened about an hour later I no longer felt sick, I felt wet. Water was lapping against my bunk. I worked the pump for about twenty minutes, until the bottom boards were dry, but it was obvious we were making water fast. No leak was visible inside the hull and the weather was worsening rapidly.

Our charts were soaked and any navigation would have to be from memory and the odd rescued scrap of soggy chart. We sighted a fishing vessel. I called him up on 2182 KHz and discovered that he was French and was using that frequency for conversation with a friend. I managed to make myself heard with the aid of the alarm button, explained our plight and requested a position. They treated this as a joke, mimicking the sound of the alarm. I shall not dwell on this, except to record that it happened.

The leak was getting worse, so was the weather. We hove to while I furled the mainsail and replaced the working jib with the storm jib. As I was returning to the cockpit, the yacht rolled heavily and I was knocked on the head by the boom. It was a sickening blow and I fell on to the cockpit sole. I remember trying to break my fall and, although I thought I got up again, it seems I lay there stunned for several minutes while Tracy, with a correct sense of priority, examined me to see that I was still breathing and left me there while she made sure the boat was all right. Nor was I particularly refreshed when I did get up. On the contrary, I was sick and a little irrational. I gave a few course instructions, which Tracy wisely ignored, and returned to my bunk.

The situation was grave. We were somewhere to the south of Ireland in a sinking yacht with an injured skipper, during a gale that was to become a storm. When I recovered my senses sufficiently, I sent out a Mayday on the Callbuoy radio. All I heard in reply were three more Mayday calls from other vessels in distress. The air was full of urgent evidence that we were not the only crew caught out. Then the earth wire of the radio parted. Despite its lead sinker, it had been blown out horizontally by the force of the gale and had snagged around the propeller of the raised outboard. This rendered useless both the radio and the engine.

There was now a full gale from the north and we had no choice but to run off before it. Cornwall lay far to the south and the North Cornish coast is a place to be feared in a northerly gale. The problems of getting around Land's End with no charts were overshadowed by the knowledge that we would not survive long enough to get there. We were cold, wet and weary and we would never have been able to keep pumping her out that long.

The loss of Gwendoline

Even with the outboard, motoring against that gale was out of the question. We had on board a Hutchinson inflatable, but with the wind shrieking across the deck I do not believe we could have secured the dinghy, even if we had succeeded in pumping it up. It would have flown like a kite.

I brought the outboard into the cockpit. It was a Seagull, and removing the propeller would not be too difficult. I went below to get some tools and, as I was on my knees and out of sight of my crew, I said a few prayers. I am afraid my maker only hears from me when I am in trouble. I needed Him then. I was frightened, sick, and feeling the weight of my responsibility for involving another person. As I later discovered, Tracy had taken advantage while I was below to say a few words herself. It was not that we were embarrassed, but rather that neither of us wished to damage the other's morale.

A few minutes later, while I was engaged in removing the propeller, the miracle happened. Tracy sighted another yacht. It appeared out of the mist and spray about three-quarters of a mile off the starboard bow and crossing our course.

I went below for the flares and grabbed two Icarus rockets. The other yacht, a large ketch-rigged Westerly, was already disappearing off the port bow as I braced myself in the forehatch and took aim. My plan was to explode the rocket above the other vessel so it would parachute down in her vicinity, since her skipper could hardly be expected to notice a red flare the best part of a mile upwind and up-spray.

The first rocket streamed in a beautiful trajectory, but carried away to the right. It may be of some use to the reader, should you ever be in a similar position, to know that initially at least the rocket turned *into* the wind. This is the opposite to what one would expect, although once in stable flight it does get carried downwind.

Correcting my aim, I fired a second rocket which flared above the other yacht's cockpit. He could not have failed to have seen it, but yet the ketch sailed on and disappeared. I began to feel very guilty about bringing Tracy along, and was starting to say as much when she pointed into the distance. The ketch was motoring towards us.

A cruising anthology

It turned out that her steering gear had been damaged by the storm and the crew had rigged an emergency tiller in the after cabin before turning her about and very gallantly returning to our aid.

The skipper was understandably reluctant to risk coming alongside in such violent conditions, but when I explained through the hailer just how bad the situation was he agreed to take us aboard.

We kept both boats sailing and as we came alongside I told Tracy to be ready to jump. Typically, she had offered to let me go first and before agreeing to obey orders and precede the skipper she extracted a promise that I would not remain aboard to try and save my boat. She got her promise, together with the threat of a thick ear if she hesitated and on the word, and as the decks were coming level, she jumped. Friendly hands pulled her to safety.

When I jumped the boats were separating so I did not quite make it. I missed the top guardrail, caught the second and smashed my knees against the hull. The sea closed over my head. Finally I looked over the rail and everyone rushed to haul me aboard. Unfortunately, they got my arms either side of a mizzen shroud and confused my reluctance to be sawn in two with saturated body weight, or perhaps narcosis of the deep. They pulled harder until finally I managed to get one arm free of its tug of war team and I shot around the stay and over the rail like a cork from a bottle.

The skipper was a doctor. He examined me and diagnosed concussion. We were given mugs of coffee, hot soup, and a couple of berths.

Norman and Sheila, and their son and nephew, were making for Penzance. The two boys had been carrying on, although seasick and needing to rest, and had stood watch for some time. I was asked if I would be up to standing a watch. Norman came into the forecabin to ask this while I was in my bunk. Tracy was asleep on the opposite bunk and I think I must have slept for a while too, because I felt much better.

That night Norman and I sailed through the worst conditions either of us had ever experienced. He decided to try to make some easting, in the hope of getting a lee from St David's head, with a

142

view to making Milford Haven.

The wind, I believe, reached a steady Force 10 and was gusting over that. Most of the night it would have been about Force 8. The seas crashed into the cockpit and several times I awakened from dozing on the sole to find myself afloat in my life-jacket, tethered by my harness and still in the cockpit. When the tiny jib was caught aback, such was the force of the wind that the deck vibrated up and down visibly. At times there was a complete 'white-out' when the air was full of brilliant white spray and you couldn't tell up from down, or sea from sky; only the gimballed compass giving any indication of the horizontal. It was a nightmare.

Like most nightmares it ended with the morning. The wind eased and we closed the coast. One of the boys took the helm and I collapsed into my bunk. At noon I awoke to find we were picking up a mooring at Milford.

We took our leave of this family of quiet and hardy people with just a brief exchange of thanks and courtesies. We shall never forget them.

Once ashore, hunger took over and we headed for the smell of steak and chips. It was a nice restaurant, I think Tracy had a cheese salad. Full marks to the waitress whose face betrayed nothing in the way of a reaction to our appearance. Tracy wasn't too bad, but as we left I caught sight of myself in a mirror, caked with salt and dried blood on my forehead. In the pocket of my torn reefer jacket I found the brass pin from the Seagull's bracket. My thoughts went back to my last sight of *Gwendoline*, my boat, her orange storm jib still set, low in the water and sailing fast towards the open Atlantic.

Geoffrey Toye lives in Wales and is a keen yachtsman, as well as a regular contributor to canoeing, archery and shooting magazines. He has a special interest in survival techniques and is also the author of a crime thriller, Diminished Responsibility.

First ocean passage

by *Barbara Townsend*

My husband David loves sailing - and lives for it. I too have grown to love it, especially when the weather is fair, the wind is a gentle, steady breeze and there's not a lot of rushing around to do. But I greeted the prospect of crossing the Atlantic with the utmost trepidation. David's enthusiasm for an opportunity to sail a boat from Tortola, in the British Virgin Islands, back to England, was matched by that of our son, Paul, who was offered the trip as a twenty-first birthday present. Together they set about convincing me that I would love it, too.

'There can't be many women your age, Mum, who've crossed the Atlantic in a 40ft yacht.'

'If Clare Francis can do it...'

Then the tactics became less persuasive, more aggressive.

'What's the matter with you, woman, you're being offered a fortnight's holiday in the Caribbean and a trans-Atlantic cruise and anyone would think you didn't want to go.'

Eventually, reluctantly, I agreed to join the crew, privately deciding that the primary reason for my presence on board would be as chief cook. I kept to myself the recurring nightmares of towering forty-foot waves and the heroic fight for survival.

The following weeks passed in a fury of activity and preparation. Gradually, all the items we thought we would need were assembled in our sitting room – charts, pilot books, SSB radio, medical kit, life jackets, wet weather gear, thermal undies, not to mention the pressure cooker, my favourite potato peeler and numerous packets of easy-blend yeast. Flights were booked for the three of us, and for our other two crew members, who were to join us a few days later, via Miami and Puerto Rico, at Tortola. Our first sight of the island was on the approach to the airport. All that one ever imagines of a Caribbean island was there below us - palm-fringed beaches of white sand and luxury yachts anchored in coral-ringed coves.

Stepping onto this tropical island paradise was like going back in time thirty years. Roger, the Englishman delegated to meet us, walked across the tarmac to greet us as we stepped from the tiny plane, its propellers still spinning. The Union Flag fluttered gently from an old-fashioned flag-pole; there was no rush to bring out the baggage from the aircraft hold, no fight to join the queue for passport control and only a mild interest in our strange assortment of baggage. The Customs official, an enormous woman with a smile to match, did enquire why we thought we might need so many warm sweaters in this climate. We wondered too, since the afternoon was hot and oppressive, wrapping us in a warm, steamy blanket of sultry air.

The bags were squeezed around us and Roger's children in his Land Rover and, after stopping at his house to meet his charming wife and enjoy a few refreshing beers, we descended to Mayo Cove where 'our' boat was at anchor. *Lizzie-B*, a ketch-rigged Saga 40, lay in the now darkening waters of the cove. As we approached in Roger's dinghy, the only sounds were the steady lap of the oars, the sudden splash as a pelican dived for fish, and the hum of crickets ashore.

Over the next two weeks we prepared *Lizzie-B* for the trip: checking rigging, sails, anchors, ropes, engine and batteries; searching through lockers for spares, of which, fortunately, there were plenty; making sure the self-steering was in order, swinging the compass, scrubbing the bottom – a not unpleasant task in the cove's clear water; and purchasing provisions and a six-man life raft. But there was still time to see something of the beautiful island, its lazy way of life and its friendly people. Many evenings were spent under the tropical stars (glass of rum-and-something in hand) hearing local stories and fascinating tales of transatlantic passages from others moored in the cove.

Our two extra crew arrived and after a shake-down cruise around some of the other Virgin Islands, with evocative names like Salt, Cooper, Ginger and Fallen Jerusalem, we made our way through the Sir Francis Drake channel to Virgin Gorda – the fat virgin - from whence we took our departure on 6 May 1988.

Provisioned, watered, fuelled to the gunwales, we headed north in splendid conditions – Force 4-5 southeasterly, the sun shining, temperature in the high 70s, on a broad reach with yankee, staysail, main and mizzen all filling well. Our first destination, 900 miles away, was Bermuda. We soon settled into our system of watch-keeping – two on watch at any one time, and each person doing four hours on, four off, four on duty again and then eight hours off. In practice, at this early stage in the voyage, we all tended to be on deck during the day, just leaving those on duty to cope after dark. My impressions were that if this was ocean sailing, it was far more pleasant than I had expected; my feelings were to change as time went on, but for now I enjoyed the routine of watches, checking the log each hour, identifying a handful of the myriad of stars in the heavens, anticipating the dead-reckoning position each morning, and watching the crew enjoy my home-made bread.

We made good progress, logging over 100 miles on each of the first four days. One night, as David and I came on watch at midnight, the stars were less apparent than usual and on the port bow was an area of ominous blackness, gradually approaching, until soon the whole sky was starless. The wind increased dramatically, but the sea remained incongruously flat. Then came the rain - in less than a minute we were drenched to the skin, water pouring off the sails in torrents, running in streams inside our light waterproofs. The rain was warm, and the boat picked up her skirts and skimmed across the black sea. As quickly as it had come, the

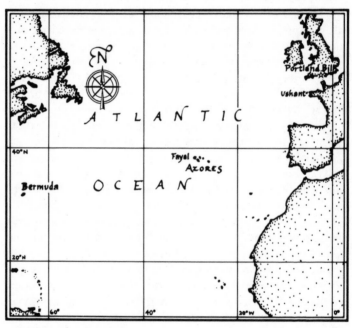

Stevens / Birthday Treat

rainstorm headed away from us and we were left shivering in the stillness, the sails dripping and flapping, the booms banging, the boat dead in the water. Daylight brought hot, burning sun, the sight of clumps of weed on the water's unruffled surface, and still air. The engine was started to charge the batteries and we chugged our way through the Sargasso Sea.

We motored on for a day and a night to within 400 miles of Bermuda, when a little breeze began to carry the heavy boat forward. The engine was switched off to conserve fuel and with dismay we realised that the 'house' batteries, which should have been well topped up by 24 hours of motoring, had not been charging at all. The alternator had failed and, as we were unable to carry out repairs at sea, it would have to be fixed in Bermuda. We spent the rest of the first leg using torchlight, to save our failing batteries for the Satnav and navigation lights. Bermuda crept closer, but now at only 3 or 4 knots and only 70 or 80 miles a day. Each watch seemed an eternity. On the tenth evening, having been briefed by our navigator to expect the loom from Bermuda's southern St David's light, I went on watch with eager anticipation. And, yes, there it was. It was a thrill to realise that after ten days and almost 900 miles, we had got it right. Ahead of us was this tiny island in the middle of the vast ocean; civilisation, albeit surrounded by spiky coral reefs.

We drew close enough to see the flat line of lights along the coastline, and the brilliant intermittent lights of the airport. But then, not wishing to make our approach until daybreak, we turned away eastwards to wait for daybreak, the welcoming lights, tantalisingly, receding. The course was carefully noted, so that there would be no difficulty in following a reciprocal course when we headed back for the island. Two hours later saw a cool grey dawn. The coast lights, now no more than pinpricks, quickly faded and we found ourselves some eight or nine miles off, no land visible at all, and storm clouds gathering as we turned westwards. One by one, the rest of the crew appeared on deck, all of us in wet weather gear, straining our eyes to the west for the first glimpse of the low-lying island. It grew suddenly much colder, the wind freshened and a line of black cloud rapidly approached from the south-west as we sped under main, mizzen and genoa towards the island. The rain began, gently at first, then harder, until any glimpse of land was once again obliterated. We were approaching fast now, the wind having reached Force 6, gusting 7, but with the sheeting rain stinging our eyes and streaming down our faces, we still had no clear view of the island. The storm was short-lived and as the rain eased we found ourselves, pilot book in hand, on line for the narrow channel to St George's harbour. Sails down, engine on, rain stopped. The sun greeted us warmly and my eyes took in the lush, steaming greenness of Bermuda.

Anchored in St George's Harbour, immigration and customs formalities completed, David set about trying to repair the faulty alternator, while I went ashore in search of shower, shops, laundrette and telephone kiosk. My tasks were easy, compared with David's. He struggled, with the help of the rest of the crew, for three days to come to terms with the boat's strange wiring system. Twice he thought he had solved it, only to have the second and third new alternators burn out again. Finally, with the help of 'Big Bob', a Bermudian, it was fixed. One more day ashore to visit Hamilton (in the rain) and celebrate Paul's 21st birthday; final purchases, phone calls home, up anchor and we were off . . . or were we? Smoke issuing from the engine compartment told us that something major was wrong – a burnt-out starter motor. Though we'd not previously come across it, we understood that there was a spare on board. A two-day search and two phone calls to the boat's owner revealed its amazing hiding place. David, once again with his head in the engine compartment, plus help from Paul and advice from the others, got it going and this time we really were leaving. The Azores were 1,800 miles away. My old fears surfaced again. While it was just a trip from the Caribbean to Bermuda, there was always the thought at the back of my mind that if I didn't like it, I could fly home from Bermuda. But this was the real thing, the real crossing. A swell on leaving Bermuda, combined with a diesel spillage and my great apprehension, saw me very sick for a day or so, but confidence returned as we clocked up 130, 140, even 150 miles a day. Within a week we were half-way. If we kept this up . . . but surely we wouldn't . . . we'd reach the Azores 'high' and there would be no wind at all. But a soldier's wind kept up for us from the south-west, so we were on

a steady broad reach for days. On two days, mid-Atlantic squalls blew up and we reduced sail, but even so we logged 168 miles on each of those days, bringing our average up to 150 miles per day. The routine continued, the bread-making continued, the grey skies continued. The eight hours off became precious, and if you didn't, or couldn't, sleep in that period, you became irritable – I know I did, and I think we were all affected. I felt some days that we were galloping along, and the hope that the crossing wouldn't take as long as the three weeks we had anticipated was beginning to become a reality. Just twelve days after leaving Bermuda, we woke one brilliant sunlit morning to the majestic sight of Mount Pico, still some 30 miles distant, rising through the heat haze. Then there were dolphins playing round the boat, almost guiding us the last few miles to the safety of Horta's harbour.

What a contrast from bustling, tourist-orientated, expensive Bermuda. Horta is a beautiful little town which you can walk around in less than half an hour. The marina is a fascinating and colourful place, with its wall paintings left by visiting yachts. One of the first ports of call in the town has to be Pete's bar – a crowded, lively meeting place for locals and yachties alike. Pete is postmaster, telephonist, and money-changer as well as barman.

Five days later we left with a forecast of strongish northeasterly winds circulating round a high, which was giving glorious June weather in England. The northeasterlies were just what we didn't want, because it meant having to tack and, with the pointing ability of *Lizzie-B* being not much better than 60 degrees off the wind, it meant slow progress home. More than 24 hours after leaving we could still see the lights of Horta, though we had done long tacks of 20 or 30 miles. Dolphins joined us again, but whales proved more photogenic, though less friendly. Early one morning, David was scrubbing the decks and suddenly heard a snort. Looking up, he saw a whale about 50 metres away from the boat. Fascinated, he watched as it slowly submerged and was gone. Other whales, in small groups of two or three, were visible in the distance.

Progress was very slow on this leg of the voyage. If we weren't headed by northeasterlies, we were almost totally becalmed. One night, the sea was so flat calm that you could see stars reflected in the water. Bursts of motoring, perhaps four hours one day, six the next, kept the average speed up to about 80 miles a day, but because of the big tacks we had made we were adding several hundred miles to the journey. A day or two playing with the spinnaker put a few more welcome miles under our belts. By now we were all tired and, in turn, bored, lonely, frustrated with the slowness and impatient to reach Falmouth. One night, twiddling with the radio, suddenly loud and clear came the Shipping Forecast, followed by Rule Britannia. That's the moment when I felt we were almost home.

As we neared the Western Approaches, the wind picked up, but again headed us, so more tacks towards Ireland, back towards Brittany. A big bang one morning alarmed us, but turned out to be Concorde breaking the sound barrier. We were getting close. The frequency of shipping increased, indeed, one massive container ship almost ran us down as she overtook; only by starting our engine and quickly manoeuvring out of her way did we avoid a collision. Finally, reckoning we were within striking distance of Falmouth under engine, we hauled down the sails and headed towards Cornwall. I was going to enjoy the sight of those green rolling hills of England, but I was denied the pleasure, since the whole of the south-west was swathed in mist.

It's never over, you're never finished in yachting, until you are safely moored, or tied alongside in a safe harbour. So, all the crew were alert in anticipation of arrival, as we navigated up the channel and safely into Falmouth. Seventeen days on the last leg – 39 days at sea in total.

No hardships, no bad weather, no fighting for survival, yet the sense of achievement was overwhelming. The following morning, travelling by train to London to meet my daughter, I felt like shouting down the railway carriage 'I've just sailed across the Atlantic!'

Barbara Townsend has been sailing for more than 23 years, starting in dinghies and progressing, via a Drascombe Lugger, to a Westerly Centaur and Westerly Fulmar.

Happy hour rescue

by *Ian Baker*

As a first-time skipper in a Tall Ships Race, I hadn't expected to get involved in a rescue – let alone the rescue of a Fastnet entrant. But it taught me some valuable lessons.

We were competing in a Channel Tall Ships race, and the weather was fabulous. The sea was calm, with just enough wind to keep us moving at 4 or 5 knots. The pressure on the skipper was minimal and that suited me just fine. *Ocean Venture*, our 60ft schooner, was beating through the sea, up the Channel towards Wolf Rock, on course for Cherbourg the long way round. *Ocean Venture* hardly heeled at all. The log kept clicking off the miles. The only sound from deck was the gentle tapping of ropes in a light breeze and the mate of the watch shouting at the helmsman for luffing. All was as usual on a sail training yacht.

The afternoon before, we had started the race just off Weymouth on the same day that the Fastnet race started. Since our gun had gone off four hours after theirs, the leaders of the Fastnet were already up to us. We had a ringside seat as Admiral's Cup entries and Tall Ships tacked up the inside of Portland Bill with a foul tide.

Happy hour rescue

It was quite something to see these modern yachts tacking to-gether with square-riggers and yesterday's schooners. We waved at all of them. Only the Swedes waved back. It seemed to us that the rest banged their wellies grumpily on the sides.

The next day, Sunday, was a carbon copy of the first. The crew were all settled well into the passage. Tea and sleep at every op-portunity. Learning the gentle art of light weather sailing. Making sure that no competitor got past us.

As we approached the Lizard we were engaged in a close match with *Helen Mary R*, the London Sailing Project's beautiful Bowman 50. This competition had started at about lunchtime, when *Ocean Venture* on port tack was crossed by *Helen Mary* on starboard, less than a boat length ahead. This pleased us no end as she had to give us quite a bit of time on handicap. All afternoon we had been close together; it's very good for crew performance to have someone to measure your speed against.

As we had both missed the tidal gate round the Lizard, we were still together, short-tacking up the east side of the Lizard just out of the tide. It was a stunning evening, and everyone was looking forward to the forthcoming night sail under full moon. We had to keep working at the tacks, and were eager to do so, looking forward to a long tack out to Wolf Rock when the tide turned.

We were allowing ourselves one can of lager each night just before the evening meal. One of the crew had just pointed out to me, rather forcibly, that it was now Happy Hour. Off he went to get fourteen cans of beer. At exactly that moment, someone on deck shouted that they had seen a red flare.

There, right under the cliffs, was a small yacht, sails in disarray, with a large red flare hanging in the sunset above her. *Ocean Venture*'s jib came down and her engine went on at full revs.

We were soon in no doubt that this was the vessel that had let off the flare. In a very short time there was an orange smoke flare on the sea, another red flare and a man on the foredeck waving his arms up and down in textbook style.

We did not take long to come up to them. The boat was *Stradivarius*, a rather pretty French quarter-tonner competing in the Fastnet. Her varnished wood sides struck one immediately as unusual in a racing boat. Unfortunately, she was very low in the

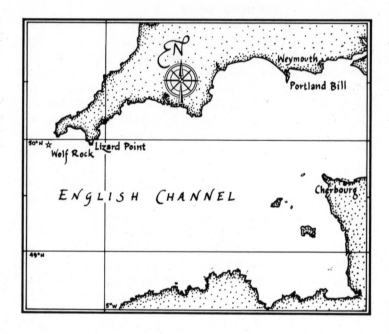

water. Her skipper had also been cheating the tide around the Lizard and was almost round when he went too close in and hit a large rock.

We were fortunate that it was early evening as all the crew were awake and alert. Furthermore, although we started off quite close to the Lizard cliffs, the tide was pushing us away from danger, out into the Channel.

The sea was so flat that we were able to come up to the yacht and tie up alongside, as if we were in a marina. There were none of the textbook troubles. We just parked next to him, with lots of fenders. So here we were, tied up to a sinking French quarter-tonner, with six very shocked Frenchmen on board who did not speak English any better than we spoke French. I can get any of the things that I require in a French hostelry (beer is a pretty universal word). I can even understand the Harbourmaster when he tells me to berth in such and such a place (but not when he tells me that I can't berth there). However, to find out from a tired, shocked French yachtsman where his yacht is holed, and what he wants to do is a completely different matter.

In the event, he made it quite clear what he wanted to do as they all leaped on board *Ocean Venture* with their kit bags. I can only say that the way you can strip a sinking boat in well under five minutes is most impressive. In no time at all we had every-thing needed to equip a competitive quarter-tonner on our deck, from sails to VHF, from oilskins to anchors.

In the meantime, I had been radioing Falmouth Coastguard, who had organised a helicopter to bring us a pump. The heli-copter was soon there, and with it a complete loss of control of the situation. I was prepared to take the sails down, but not for the mind-numbing noise that the helicopter brought with it. From a situation where everything was calm and easy, we were swept up in the whirling maelstrom of the chopper blades. The crew were distracted from their jobs and could not hear the shouted orders.

The first helicopter to arrive disgorged a diver. He swam across to us and climbed aboard. By this time the first mate was aboard *Stradivarius*, bailing with a bucket and our washing-up bowl. A second helicopter arrived with a pump. This was passed with ease

down a line into the quarter-tonner's cockpit.

Eventually we got the pump's petrol engine started and, although it stopped a couple of times for no reason at all, it began to make headway on the leak.

To add to the air of unreality, the Lizard lifeboat appeared at about this time. It later transpired that it was taking local dignitaries on a trip around the bay, but at the time the sight of a lifeboat foredeck packed with well-dressed ladies and gentlemen only added to the noisy confusion. After some conversation with the lifeboat coxswain and the French sailors (talking in English was by now just as difficult as miming in French), we loaded the French crew and their belongings into the middle of the foredeck party on the lifeboat. The sight of a cotton print dress completely wrapped in a Mylar mainsail is worth seeing. Then we passed *Stradivarius* into the tender care of the RNLI and took the diver onto *Ocean Venture*. There was still one helicopter there to take him away. Once the lifeboat had gone, quarter-tonner in tow, the diver said goodbye and casually jumped into the water, where the helicopter would lower him a strop. We hoisted sail and, against all instincts, sailed away from him. On his way up into the hovering helicopter he did a little ballet on wire for us.

Within three minutes, we were close-hauled on starboard tack in blessed silence, heading for the Lizard, wondering if it had really happened.

'Can we have Happy Hour *now*, skipper?'

Ian Baker is an electronics engineer who has sailed extensively in United Kingdom waters as a relief skipper with the Ocean Youth Club. He is also a Yachtmaster instructor. As a result of the incident described in Happy hour rescue, Ocean Venture *was voted the Cutty Sark Trophy at the end of the Tall Ships Race.*

Over my shoulder

by *Ronnie Andrews*

In the history of cruising, particularly during the twenty years between the world wars, one can find excerpts from old logs which catch the essence, the soul, of that cruising scene.

Nearly all good cruises in those days were made either without or with the minimum of internal combustions. A standard of one horsepower per Thames ton was accepted by designers, and it was only towards the end of the inter-war era that the belief slowly faded that yacht engines were faintly vulgar. The introduction of diesels, and the attendant improvement of reliability and design, doubtless speeded up the arrival of a new era. In the process, I am certain that we have all lost something of both the enjoyment and the art of cruising.

It is quite difficult to realise how much things have changed in 50 years. Yachts were then much larger and paid hands were not a rarity. The maintenance of the heavy gear seemed endless; drying heavy cotton sails, fighting mildew, reeving off new manila sheets (not expected to last more than one season), sweating up the tarred hemp shroud lanyards, and having always to moor with two anchors when fetching up, to avoid fouling the big fisherman anchor, 'old cold nose'.

It was still the era of tarred cordage and plough steel, of marlinespikes and the inimitable smell in chandlers' stores. There was a more leisurely, a more courtly feeling, one of setting topsails, heaving-to each morning for a cold bath with buckets of seawater, of going to church on Sundays. Harbourmaster and boatmen were willing, there was room to anchor in harbour and dues, if any, were minimal. One even supplemented a very limited variety in the diet with sides of smoked bacon, cutting off the rind and using it to grease the mast against the friction of the hoops.

Dinghies of large and heavy size were generally towed with two painters, and more often than not lost in bad weather. It was not unusual with those large dinghies to have to tow the yacht, with several oarsmen rowing out of time so the tow-rope never slacked up.

The reference books of those days were *The Complete Yachtsman*, by Heckstall-Smith, *Yacht Cruising* and *Yacht Voyaging*, by Claude Worth, and the Lonsdale Library *Cruising*. Reed's Almanac cost four shillings.

The first published log of a cruise in a small vessel to the southward of the Raz de Sein was that of Claude Worth's first *Tern*, in 1896. It was then generally considered a foolhardy venture, although a more ambitious voyage that he had made the previous year around Great Britain passed without comment. Worth's industry was amazing. Beside his Harley Street practice and work at Moorfields he found time to write books and would rise daily and work from 5am to 8 am on the design of *Tern III*, making detailed scale drawings of every bit of ironwork and feature aboard. In 1926 his was the first British yacht to visit the Azores.

In those days one could see a fleet of twenty Brixham Trawlers with everything set working out to sea off the Start. I once counted 120 fishing craft under sail within my horizon in the Baie de Douarnenez. It was getting towards the end of such sights. By 1939 the Tunny fleet was already installing engines. One feels a sense of loss.

Circumnavigations were made, prior to the opening in 1914 of the Panama canal, by Slocum and Voss and, in considerable contrast, by the Brasseys, in their 157ft, three-masted gaff schooner, *Sunbeam*. Her steam auxiliary engine used four tons of coal a day and on sailing from Valparaiso, bound towards Tahiti, they loaded six sheep, sixty chickens, thirty ducks and forty-eight pigeons for the five-week passage.

After 1918, world cruises were soon in vogue. Ralph Stock in his 47ft Colin Archer cutter got as far as Tonga; his previous experience included a year aboard a Brixham Trawler and a voyage from Sydney towards Norfolk Island when 'we were wrecked before our dictionary of sea-terms could be much improved'.

His navigation in *Ogre* still seemed a bit odd when, on 1 May 1920, in the Pacific, he wrote, 'We hove-to in half a gale, but in perfect comfort, until, at dawn, we discovered that by some miracle we had drifted into the circle of reefs from which there was no visible outlet. There was apparently surf on every hand, and all we could do was to sail and motor clean round the reef until we came to an exit, which we at last did, though it was little more than twenty yards wide'.

Muhlhauser's world cruise in *Amarylis* seems to have been the next, in 1923, two years before Conor O'Brien sailed round south of the three capes with his two paid hands. He took two years to the minute to sail home to Ireland, despite a three-month stop in harbour in the Falklands, when he took a steamer passage to the South Shetlands and Graham's Land. 'I still regard anything to the east of Cape Horn as home waters'.

It was also at that time that Cdr R D Graham was sailing his 4-ton cutter *Onaway*, with his then teenaged daughter, Helen Tew. Typical of the discomfort accepted as normal in those days is his description of being hove-to in the Irish sea: 'I retired to the cabin to put on a mac, instead of my useless oilskins. The cabin floor was just awash and it seemed useless to change into dry clothes. Getting a bit cold, I took off my mac and rolled up in a blanket, taking a peep out now and again to see all was clear. Unluckily, the primus had capsized and emptied its contents, so the bilge water washing about the cabin smelt very much of paraffin and made me feel a bit squeamish.' He later made a famous early North Atlantic crossing in *Emanuel*, growing anti-scorbutic mustard and cress on blotting paper.

In a similar vein, H R Wallace, in his engineless 5-ton gaff cutter, *Marie*, sailed around Great Britain. 'All deck seams pour water, everything is soaked; one expects this in a small boat, so why complain. Woke from an extraordinarily vivid dream to find water all over the floor boards, and to see the top of a big one come boarding down the companion steps. What a life! Lit lamp and bailed the cabin and gybed ship onto the port tack, heading NNW. As my usual canvas shoes were waterlogged, I looked in the locker for my Sunday-go-to-meeting brogues. They were there all right – full to the top with cold North Sea. Becalmed now five miles north of the Maidens Rock; dead calm, I'm not. A night of profound stillness. A magnificent full moon looks down, roars with laughter and asks my opinion of auxiliary motors.'

Having crossed a number of oceans myself since reaching three score years and ten, I realise how much more comfortable life aboard has become. It used to be considered that by 69 one was 'a man long past the age when the spice of romance seasons the dough of discomfort'.

Life seemed to be a great deal more of an adventure. Even to race round the Fastnet rock was, in 1925, considered by some as highly questionable seamanship, which would provoke letters to *The Times*. In those days, it was by modern standards more a cruise in company.

We take so much for granted these days. Valve wireless sets, if taken at all, were most unreliable, shipping forecasts a rarity until 1933, when Daventry gave the weather and Rugby the time. RDF did not get into its stride until after the war. Bermudian rig started in the early thirties, while CQR anchors were just in time for the war, invented by Prof G I Taylor, the owner of *Frolic*, a Bristol Channel Pilot Cutter. Early tests were made in the Shetlands in 1934, when his friend, G McKerrow, found that he could replace the 70 lb fisherman aboard his 31ft sloop with a 35 lb CQR: 'A tremendous boon' and who would not agree?

I have tremendous respect for single-handers who competed in the OSTAR. Vast as some of their craft have been, they have the advantage of modern gear; the earlier single-handers seem to have been even tougher. Admiral L Goldsmith's heavy cutter, *Rame*, set 1,300sq ft and crossed a square yard, in 1927. She also had a

two-ton lead keel, seven tons of inside ballast, and stowed a ton of water and 80 gallons of paraffin.

Description of heavy weather over the years show that our problems remain essentially the same, but some people have a better ability to describe it. In 1930 Nigel Warrington-Smyth, in the 51ft ex-Barry Pilot Gutter *Gariad*, wrote: 'Hove-to in the Bay of Biscay. It was a terrible night, very thick with flying spindrift... crouching in the cockpit and gazing at the towering heights that roared down upon us we pondered the universe as suggested by Sir James Jeans, endeavouring to picture his four-dimensional continuum bending back upon itself so that space became finite. We failed, as others had failed before us, as we rose to each crest we could see no further than the two dimensional surface of the sea, which bending forward on itself in threatening rushes, gave us the unpleasant feeling that it might be infinite.'

This was the storm during which some twenty French Tunnymen were lost, in collisions off Ushant and by running for the hoped-for safety of harbour.

It was from necessity that Captain Goldsmith, as he was in 1928, had to sail *Rame* home from Malta in December, with two friends. Owing to appalling weather, they only made Ferol. In his inimitable way he describes how they weathered one dreadful gale off the coast of Portugal, only to meet another when 180 miles to the westward of Cavo Villano.

'Midnight, *Rame* getting out of hand. Barometer falling steeply – steeper than in all my experience I've seen it fall. Reefed still more, and then, choosing my moment, brought her to the wind without shipping a drop and hove-to. This gale has killed us almost. We have given up all hope of England and are hoping some day to make Ferol and lay up. Our misery is so great that I think we have reached the uttermost point. The floor boards are awash. The fury of the wind and sea is absolutely stunning. How old *Rame* stands up to it I can't think. She is a perfect marvel. The gear seems well enough yet, but I spent a deadly time in the forecastle, under a pile of soaking sails, hauling out the sea anchor and its warp, all ready.

'My word, last night was a terror. What a perfect fool I was to gamble with the unconquered sea like this. You should see the trace of the barograph, and see the hungry, cold, pitiless sea *Rame* is battling with.'

One could quote the Admiral indefinitely, but read the old RCC Journals and judge for yourself. I leave the last words to him: 'Down tumbles the glass, and slosh comes the vile rain from black and menacing clouds, but there! This wandering life alone suits me. I have a delightful sense of being born again to youth, the world is more buoyant with bright illusions. Existence is as fresh as it was thirty years ago, and once more a bubble, iridescent with all the colours of hope.'

Dr Ronnie Andrews, who describes himself as 'a retired medico', lives in Sydney, Australia and at 82 is still actively sailing. His 33ft teak Buchanan designed yacht, Alcestè, *is his sixth boat. He undertook a circumnavigation in* Merlin *in 1969-71 and made a passage, when aged 72, to Australia with his family in his present yacht. An ex-Commodore of the Royal Cruising Club and a member of the RORC for 16 years, he has contributed numerous articles to yachting magazines.*